Praise for *Blogging for*

"I've been told that the glory ⟨ ⟩ ...ging are long gone. Maybe. What I am sure of is that blogging is now a crowded field, filled with countless voices offering pathways to success. I've longed for voices like Benjamin and John's, filled with seasoned wisdom and an unwavering resolve to elevate the glory of God over all other aims. Forged out of the hard hours of reading carefully, working the keyboards, and humbly connecting with other writers, this book proves that Benjamin and John are fast becoming two voices to heed in whatever lies ahead."

> **Chris Thomas,** pastor of Raymond Terrace Community Church in the Hunter Valley of NSW, Australia, host of the Gospel-Centered Discipleship Writers' Guild, and blogger at PloughmansRest.com

"Ok, I'll admit it: blogging isn't dead. And I wouldn't want to kill it. But blogging has changed, because nothing ever lasts long on the internet. John and Benjamin are reliable guides to how you can still blog to the glory of God. I'm praying God will use their book to help raise up a new generation of writers eager to use their gifts to tell the world about the good news of Jesus Christ."

> **Collin Hansen,** editorial director of The Gospel Coalition, host of the Gospelbound podcast, and author of *Blind Spots* and *Young, Restless, Reformed*

"Writing is a lonely endeavor. With this book Benjamin Vrbicek and John Beeson create a needed community. Reading it is to sit around a table with other writers, sharing tips and tricks of the trade, as well as deeper issues like prioritizing God's glory and staying spiritually vital throughout the seasons of writing and ministry. I heartily invite all bloggers to pull up a chair and join in this helpful conversation."

> **Jen Oshman,** author of *Enough About Me*, former overseas missionary, pastor's wife, podcaster, and blogger at JenOshman.com

"Writing for online, public consumption is a tricky thing for Christians. We fight pride when pageviews soar *and* when they tank. Throw in tech problems, networking, and unfriendly algorithms, and it's easy to lose sight of our purpose in writing. *Blogging for God's Glory in a Clickbait World* offers a primer for launching a blog and a heart check for sustaining it. Immensely practical and engaging, this book is for bloggers of every age and stage. Though I've been blogging for nearly two decades, I finished this book with renewed purpose to make much of Christ in my own small corner of the internet. *Blogging for God's Glory* is a book I'll recommend over and over to aspiring writers."

Glenna Marshall, author of *The Promise is His Presence* and *Everyday Faithfulness*, and blogger at GlennaMarshall.com

"My advice to any Christian who is thinking about starting a blog is to first read this book—and to pay close attention. Vrbicek and Beeson have written the most helpful and realistic guide to Christian blogging that has been produced in a decade. If you follow their advice (and examine your true motives) they can save you a lot of wasted time and frustration by showing you why your sole objective should be to blog for the glory of God."

Joe Carter, Executive Pastor of McLean Bible Church, editor at The Gospel Coalition, and coauthor of *How to Argue like Jesus*

Blogging for God's Glory in a Clickbait World

foreword by **Tim Challies**

BLOGGING *for* **GOD'S GLORY** *in a* CLICKBAIT **WORLD**

Benjamin Vrbicek & John Beeson

Blogging for God's Glory in a Clickbait World

© 2020 Benjamin Vrbicek & John Beeson

A publication of FAN AND FLAME Press in Harrisburg, Pennsylvania

All rights reserved. No part of this book may be reproduced or transmitted in any form or by any means whatsoever without express written permission from the authors, except in the case of brief quotations embodied in critical articles and reviews.

Cover & interior design: Benjamin Vrbicek

Paperback ISBN: 978-1-7348-4942-4
Ebook ISBN: 978-1-7348-4943-1

Scripture quotations are from The ESV® Bible (The Holy Bible, English Standard Version®), copyright © 2001 by Crossway, a publishing ministry of Good News Publishers. 2016 Text Edition. Used by permission. All rights reserved.

for those about to blog, we salute you

CONTENTS

CONTENTS

H istory has not recorded who started the very first blog, but I rather imagine some intrepid writer around the turn of the millennium was feeling rather chuffed after beginning a little site where he could share some of his interests on this neat, new medium called the Internet. He jotted down a few articles, wrote a book review or two, and shared some opinions on politics. And I expect that in his pride and excitement he soon showed it to someone else—a friend perhaps. "I call it a blog," he said. At which point he undoubtedly heard the words that have been said about blogs ever since: "Don't you know that blogs are dead?"

The fact is, prophets and prognosticators have forecast the death of the blog since it was little more than a twinkle in some clever programmer's eye. Birthed at a time where we were just gaining universal access to the World Wide Web, a time before we had ever heard of "Twitter,"

"Facebook," or "Instagram," (or iPhone, for that matter) blogs were the social media of the early 2000s. They were groundbreaking in the way they democratized the ability to create information and shape conversations. The old gate-keepers of print, radio, and television suddenly had to contend with a million voices on a million blogs. It changed everything.

But, of course, other social media platforms soon sprang up and gained stunning popularity. Where there may have been millions of blogs, there were billions of Facebook accounts. The sounds of the bells grew louder as they tolled for the death of the blog.

But it's not quite so simple. Time has proven that new forms of social media may *dis*place many blogs, but they cannot fully *re*place them. Twitter is limited by its character count, Facebook by its emphasis on urgency and its near-to-talitarian data policies, Instagram by its emphasis on images. If each of these platforms has a place, surely blogs do as well, perhaps especially among Christians. If you ask me, I say the future is bright! And as we consider a new generation of blogs and bloggers, I'm thankful to be able to recommend *Blogging for God's Glory in a Clickbait World*. It will prove a sure and steady guide to the past, present, and future of Christian blogging.

Tim Challies
pastor, author, blogger

Introduction

Benjamin Vrbicek

ALIGNING OUR MOTIVATIONS

What Does It Mean to Blog for God's Glory?

D addy, I painted this for you," says my daughter Izzy. Closing the door behind me and setting my work bag on the table, I bend over to look at the paper she's covered with splotches of primary colors in the shape of people. The paper is still wrinkly from liberally applied paint. She places her artwork in my hand.

"That's wonderful," I say, trying to figure out which way is up and which is down. I've learned from experience not to ask, "What is this?" Instead I say, "Tell me about your picture, sweetie."

"It's a doggie in our backyard, and all of our family is eating pickles," she says.

"Oh, I see. May I hang it on the fridge?"

Izzy smiles wide. Her two front teeth are missing.

We hang her wrinkly artwork on the front of our refrigerator along with all the others.

People tend to mark the stages of life. We save the paystub from our first paychecks, mount diplomas on walls, celebrate a marriage and a first mortgage. I'm in that stage of life where my fridge hides behind artwork from my children. They hand me watercolor paintings when I leave for work. They hand me colored-pencil drawings when I come home from work. They come to work to hand me colored macaroni glued to construction paper. It's wonderful. I don't want it to end.

What I love most is the innocence of their gifts. My little Izzy doesn't have a clue there is such a place as the British Museum housing works of Rembrandt and Rubens. Izzy doesn't know anything about the Louvre in Paris that displays da Vinci's *Mona Lisa* for ten million visitors each year. All Izzy knows is our fridge: the two sides of the fridge and the front side of the fridge. I guess we could call them the three sides of our art galleries. The front of our fridge—or the main gallery, if you will—receives nearly ten visits a day, or maybe one hundred visits a day in the summer when our children enjoy vacation and standing in front of an open fridge. But no one in our family visits the fridge necessarily to see her artwork. That's the child-like innocence Izzy has when we mount her paintings. If an adult were to possess this kind of ignorance of the great works of art, especially an adult given to producing her own art, we'd call it something other than innocence; her ignorance would take on the pejorative, culpable sense of the word. In a child, however, the ignorance is admirable.

The purity of her gifts strikes me too. "Daddy, I painted this *for you*," she says. Izzy paints not for fame or money or from the overflow of competition with her siblings, but *for you*, she says. When I say purity, I mean this kind of single-mindedness, the kind of joy that is captivated by and treasures only the smile of her father. No mixed motives, no duplicity. Only pure, single-minded devotion.

I'm not saying children are innocent and pure and full of rainbows and bubble gum. I believe in original sin because I read of it in the Bible and also because I see it in the mirror and in the eyes of every one of my young children who—if their little arms were strong enough—might kill me rather than not get their way. Children are not pure and innocent in an absolute sense. As those downstream from our father Adam, we are not sinners because we sin, but we sin because we are sinners. As David writes, "In sin did my mother conceive me" (Ps 51:5).

Still, I think about my children's artwork often when I blog. I like to think of God printing out my blog posts and hanging them on his heavenly fridge, which I'm sure is huge and made of stainless steel and has an ice dispenser that always works. I like to think of God stooping over to smile and say, "Tell me about this one, Benjamin." I like to think God has a big big house with lots and lots of room and a big big fridge where he can host my blog.

Again, I hope these sentiments don't betray my foolishness or ignorance or even my arrogance. I know my blog posts are only feeble and flimsy collections of words, while J. I. Packer's book *Knowing God* has gravitas. I know that though the internet keeps a record of all my blog posts, should the Lord tarry, Augustine's *Confessions* will still be read in AD 3020 while my posts will be long forgotten. I know that as I blog about some suffering that feels weighty to me, Corrie ten Boom's Holocaust survival story makes my problems appear as they really are: light and momentary. From jails, Bunyan and Bonhoeffer wrote masterpieces. And

I, from my dining room table, have the gall to expect my internet-published words should hang in the heavenly gallery?

A Mixed Bag of Motives

It's so difficult to know our own motives because they are always layered and mixed. When the mother of two disciples asked for her sons to sit at the right and left of Jesus in his kingdom (Matt 20:21), I'm inclined to think the request had less to do with wanting to be close to Jesus and more to do with being seen as close to Jesus—a subtle but significant difference. It's not clear whether the two sons of Zebedee saw their own motives. Perhaps, to them, the request seemed less worldly. Jesus, however, saw in their eyes lust for exaltation.

> I never expected blogging to so test my heart and challenge my motivations. As I write, edit, submit for feedback, and finally post publicly, every step is an opportunity to look to my own motivations, my own desire for glory, praise, and popularity.
> – Ryan Williams, *amicalled.com* [1]

Jesus then asks if they will still follow him even when they must drink his cup and undergo his baptism. The baptism and cup referred to in that passage were the way of suffering, the way of the cross, the way of honoring God when no one applauds and everyone maligns you. Will they still want to be close to Jesus when he must drink the cup of the cross before he wears the crown? There's a bloody baptism before the resurrection.

What about us? Would we still invest two hours, or even ten hours, in a blog post when the post is for God and God

---

[1] All pull-quotes from bloggers throughout the book come from email correspondence with the authors.

alone, the God who is in secret and who sees in secret (Matt 6:6)? Would we work to get a post exactly right if we knew the post would get zero traffic and zero likes? Or, maybe instead of zero traffic, what if the post gets tons of traffic and comments and shares but only by those furious with us? I'd like to think I'd still blog, but I don't know.

In his book *The Prodigal God*, Timothy Keller tells a story about our sometimes-pure and sometimes-selfish motives.[2] A gardener once gave his king his most prized carrot. "My Lord," said the gardener, "this is the greatest carrot I've ever grown or ever will grow. Therefore I want to present it to you as a token of my love and respect for you."[3] The king discerned the good in the man's heart, gladly received the carrot, and rewarded the gardener handsomely. An onlooker took note and gave the king his best horse, thinking if a carrot is thus rewarded, how much more the gift of a beautiful horse. But to the surprise of the horse giver, the king gave him no reward. Perplexed, he inquired why. "That gardener was giving *me* the carrot," the king said, "but you were giving *yourself* the horse."[4] In other words, it looked like he was honoring the king with his gift, but giving his gift was more like throwing a boomerang; he only threw it so he could catch it. Again, our motives are layered and mixed.

I fear too many times I've tricked myself into saying I'm blogging for the glory of the King of kings when I'm blogging for my own glory. I write a post for God, but deep down I'm giving myself a horse. I want God to print my post and hang it on his stainless-steel fridge but only so long as it sits in a

[2] Timothy Keller, *The Prodigal God: Recovering the Heart of the Christian Faith* (New York: Penguin, 2008), 60–62.

[3] Ibid., 61.

[4] Ibid., 61–62, emphasis original.

more prominent place than the posts of my siblings. I can't have brothers and sisters ranking higher on the fridge than me.

Why He Should Increase and Our Blogs Decrease

We need to slow down and back up. I've begged the question. That phrase—to beg the question—used to be understood differently than most understand it today. Now, when a person speaks about begging the question, they most often mean that something said naturally leads to a follow-up question. But historically, to beg the question meant to assume the truth of something by not actually arguing for that truth. For example, if you argue that running is the best exercise for your body because it burns the most calories, you have begged the question. You have assumed that what constitutes the best exercise is the exercise that burns the most calories. But *is* burning the most calories the only way we decide the best exercise? No.

What does this have to do with anything? John and I don't want to beg the question that a blogger *should* aspire to blog for God's glory. We don't want to assume what should be argued. Now, we expect that the audience who might buy this sort of book would probably track well enough with us even if we didn't explicitly argue for this aim of blogging. But still, we don't want to write a book about blogging for God's glory without actually giving time to exploring that this is what we *should* do. So, consider the way Paul begins his letter to the church in Ephesus.

> Blessed be the God and Father of our Lord Jesus Christ, who has blessed us in Christ with every spiritual blessing

in the heavenly places, even as he chose us in him before the foundation of the world, that we should be holy and blameless before him. In love he predestined us for adoption to himself as sons through Jesus Christ, according to the purpose of his will, *to the praise of his glorious grace*, with which he has blessed us in the Beloved. (Eph 1:3–6, emphasis added)

Those long and lofty sentences span God's plan from eternity past to eternity future. God's aim, Paul writes, in all that he has done—blessing Christians with spiritual gifts; orchestrating the plan whereby we might become holy before him; lovingly choosing us to be his children through adoption in Jesus; the whole plan of redemption—is "to the praise of his glorious grace." Everything about redemption—the beginning, middle, and end—aims to exalt the glory of God's grace.

> Blogging is one of God's ordinary means to encourage and grow his saints—both the writer and the reader. It's one more way to express truth, honor God, and serve others.
> – *Jen Oshman, jenoshman.com*

Consider also the way Peter puts it. "But you are a chosen race, a royal priesthood, a holy nation, a people for his own possession, that you may proclaim the excellencies of him who called you out of darkness into his marvelous light" (1 Pet 2:9). In the first movie of the *Toy Story* franchise, Andy signs his name on the bottom of Woody's foot. He did this to indicate his possession of and his love for Woody. Peter writes that Christians are special to God, as though he signed his name on our feet. God treasures blood-bought Christians. And all this, Peter says, is so that we might become those who "proclaim the excellencies of him who called [us] out of darkness into his marvelous light."

This is similar to what Jesus preached in the Sermon on the Mount. "Let your light shine before others," Jesus said. But why? Why should we live in the light of God's goodness in a dark world? Jesus continues, "so that they may see your good works and give glory to your Father who is in heaven" (Matt 5:16). The point of our shining is that others would see that the purity and power and pleasure of following God does not originate with us but from God, and in seeing God's light in us, they might praise him.

Perhaps one of the most emphatic verses about God's passion for his own glory comes from the prophet Isaiah. He writes,

> For my name's sake I defer my anger, for the sake of my praise I restrain it for you, that I may not cut you off. Behold, I have refined you, but not as silver; I have tried you in the furnace of affliction. For my own sake, for my own sake, I do it, for how should my name be profaned? My glory I will not give to another. (Isa 48:9–11)

Don't miss the repetition: *For my name's sake ... For the sake of my praise ... For my own sake, for my own sake ... My glory I will not give to another.* David wrote a similar line in our beloved Psalm 23: "The Lord is my shepherd .... He leads me in paths of righteousness for his name's sake" (23:1, 3).

In light of all these passages and the many others like them, I hope when I write about God smiling over my crop of published "carrots," that the predominant desire of my heart is the innocence and purity of a child creating art for Abba. I hope deep down my work and toil is not in order to self-promote or, in Keller's words, give myself a horse. I hope all my striving aims to obey Paul's admonition to work at everything as unto the Lord, not men (Col 3:23). I hope that more than any other motive, whether I eat or drink or blog, I do all for God's glory (1 Cor 10:31).

The Unhelpful Magnetism of Metrics

In all honesty, though, this book is going to disappoint some of you. We're sure of it. So we might as well address it sooner rather than later.

We're not writing so you'll learn the secrets to "10x-ing" the number of sales on your blog—or "7x-ing" your blog since seven is, after all, the biblical number for completeness. This book won't give you the exact email copy we used to get key influencers to endorse our work. We can't help you monetize the moment, identify your brand niche, grow your readership on trees, or make pigs fly. We're not going to do this because, quite frankly, we don't know how. I wish my email list grew like bamboo, but it doesn't.

Experienced blogger Laura Lundgren shares a similar frustration, specifically how women bloggers tend to describe success. "They all seemed to have a similar storyline: I just started writing, suddenly everyone loved my writing, and then I got a book deal!" Lundgren confesses, "I couldn't figure out how you went from having a blog only your mom read to having a book deal? I still don't know that answer."[5]

I'm not sure if you share my same fascination with the promotional videos in your Instagram feed from authors and entrepreneurs. They cast a spell over me. Often the videos are so bad I find myself unable *not* to watch. And I know

---

[5] Laura Lundgren, "God Is Doing Small Things through Me," *Little House in the Suburbs*, October 11, 2019, https://littlehouseinthesuburb.wordpress.com/2019/10/11/god-is-doing-small-things-through-me/.

how the social media algorithms work: the more I watch, the more I get. But even if you're not sucked in by their power, you've probably seen enough promotional videos to know the standard trope. Some super successful *author*preneur— the ugly portmanteau of author and entrepreneur—stands in some impressive office or on the patio of his mansion or in front of his exotic car waving his book at the camera while talking about how, despite his humble upbringing, he's now managed to generate streams of passive income that flow like the River Jordan at flood stage. Great for him. I'm glad he learned how to quit the 9–5, become his own boss, and stick it to the man. However, I can't help you live your life always up and to the right because I don't know how to do so.

> For me, the most unexpected aspect of blogging is how it's pure steroids for the narcissist, especially when people start reading, liking, and sharing your material. You think you're important and profound and an influencer. You're probably not.
> – Jeremy Writebol, *jwritebol.net*

Don't confuse my inability with the lack of desire, though. Metrics of growth have a magnetism that tugs on my heart as much as the next blogger. I want to see more pageviews this year than last year, more unique visitors, more conversions, and more shares on social media. I want to write guest posts that go viral and have readers grab my lead magnets like catnip. I want a stock-photo life.

Sure, my website has grown. I have more readers this year than the last, as was the case in each of the previous five years. The growth, however, has not been 10x, meaning 100 subscribers this year, 1,000 the next, and 10,000 the year after. My growth has been more like 1.5x with 100 subscribers this year, 150 the next, 225 the following year. After six years of blogging regularly, I only have three or four articles that generate their own Google traffic and, even then, the traffic is only a trickle.

In other words, my blog has grown the way my children do. You look at them from one day to the next and nothing changes. Nothing even changes across the fall and winter. Then spring and summer race by. Here comes fall again, and I send my children off to school on picture day, and I happen to look at their pictures from the previous year and my, oh my, how time flew and they grew without me even noticing.

The Power to Blog When Blogging Is Slogging

John and I think we know enough about blogging to help you achieve this kind of growth, the kind that is imperceptible when measured across days and most months but not so when measured in years. And if you follow the advice in this book and growth comes quicker, that's great too.

Yet more than achieving numerical growth, we want you to have the character to blog faithfully whether you see any growth at all. We want you to maintain the motivation when blogging feels more like slogging, to borrow the word Tim Challies uses to describe the grind.[6]

But where will this kind of motivation come from?

Pastor and author Zack Eswine raises this question in his book *The Imperfect Pastor*.[7] Some people conceive of pastoral ministry in a local church as doing large things famously and fast, he writes several times. It's the Western way to see our gospel kingdoms grow like the tiny mustard seed that becomes a tree for all the birds of the air. But, he argues,

---

[6] For example, Tim Challies, "Slogging Blogging," *Challies.com*, July 5, 2017, https://www.challies.com/articles/slogging-blogging/.

[7] Zack Eswine, *The Imperfect Pastor: Discovering Joy in Our Limitations through a Daily Apprenticeship with Jesus* (Wheaton: Crossway, 2015).

what if pastoral ministry is more about doing thankless deeds for a long period of time among those mostly overlooked by the world?

Most cities have a church or a few churches that have grown rapidly, just as there are plenty of examples of authors with blogs that have grown rapidly. But the ordinary church and the ordinary blog still serve God. John and I believe the only way Christian bloggers will have the stamina to do the kind of slogging that most bloggers do each week—the kind of blogging that honors God and serves a small number of mostly overlooked readers who rarely say thank you—is when we blog for God's glory, not our own.

But here's the best thing. Blogging for God's glory, in fact, doing anything for God's glory, is actually the way we get the most joy in life. Jonathan Edwards argued for this at length in his long essay called *A Dissertation Concerning the End for Which God Created the World*. If the title is a mouthful, the book is more so. Edwards argues that, spoiler alert, God created the world for his own glory. To use the language of Paul from the end of Romans 11, we could say the end for which God created the world was that we might know that from *him* and through *him* and to *him* are all things and to *him* be glory forever. The universe exists to display God's glory. But Edwards also argues that making much of God's glory is what brings us the most joy. God created us to be most satisfied when we make the most of him. Or to say it the way John Piper often does, "God is most glorified in us when we are most satisfied in him." God's aim of exalting the glory of his grace and our highest happiness are not two contradictory passions but one united passion. The theologians who drafted the Westminster Shorter Catechism wrote something similar. The first question in the catechism famously asks, "What is the chief end of man?" The answer, they say, is "to glorify God and enjoy him forever."

The stamina to blog when blogging feels like slogging comes when we find our highest joy in blogging the excellencies of him who called us into his marvelous light.

What Does It Mean to Blog for God's Glory?

Now comes perhaps the hardest question of all: What does it mean to blog for God's glory? Specifically, what does it mean to blog for God's glory in a world that loves clickbait, those posts with seductive titles and content pumped full of high-fructose corn syrup?

Definitions are difficult but essential. I remember arguing with family members about the definition of a "Christian t-shirt." At the time, my younger sister attended a Christian high school. Each Friday students were allowed to ditch their uniforms for Christian t-shirts. Not meaning to be silly or difficult, I wondered what a Christian t-shirt was. What about certain yards of cotton, cut and screen pressed with ink, makes the shirt Christian?

The options abound. Is a Christian t-shirt a shirt with a Bible verse? Or maybe a Christian t-shirt is one of those not-so-clever shirts that tweaks a popular brand logo and slogan toward something related to Christianity, like "Jesus is my *LIFE SAVIOR*." Perhaps a Christian t-shirt is a shirt made by Christians? Or perhaps it's a t-shirt worn by a Christian, and thus the unclean becomes clean by contact, as when Jesus touched lepers and made them clean? Jesus did say whoever believes in him will do "greater works than these" (John 14:22). Maybe a Christian t-shirt is one made with integrity and excellence, you know, something sourced from the finest fair-trade, free-range cotton? Not to belabor the point, but perhaps a Christian t-shirt is a shirt that has repented of its sins, put its faith in Christ, and asked God to come into its threads. That's how people become Christians—sort of, anyway.

You might be able to think of other silly or serious possibilities. It turned out, according to the administration at my sister's school, a Christian t-shirt was one with a Christian music band image on it. Of course I wanted to ask what makes a band a Christian band but, for the sake of the relationship, I let it go.

Again, definitions are essential. They helped my sister know which shirts were allowed to be worn on Fridays and which were not. Let me propose the definition of blogging for God's glory that we'll use for the rest of the book. It's a two-pronged answer. Blogging for God's glory means . . .

first, to have our motivations aligned with God's, and

second, to pursue excellence in the craft, including theological precision, beautiful prose, visual appeal, and the edification of readers, all drawing from the best industry practices.

I've talked about the first part of the definition already. To blog for God's glory means to have our motivation aligned with his, namely, to blog for the praise of his glorious grace. He must increase; we must decrease.

As for the second part of the definition, the pursuit of excellence in the craft, we'll need the rest of the book to explore what this means. So, keep going with us. Two pastors wrote a book about blogging for God's glory, and you won't believe what happened next.

Chapter 1

John Beeson

PURPOSE

Why Am I Blogging, and Who Am I Trying to Reach?

I got the itch to write when I was a fourth grader in Ms. Reeves's class. We had free writing time and once a week we read our creations to the class. I was reading J. R. R. Tolkien's *The Hobbit* for the first time and had a serious case of Middle-earth-itis. Another boy in my class had caught the Middle-earth bug as well.

We were off, each of us writing facsimiles of *The Hobbit.* Only, he had the imaginative horsepower to create something that could stand on its own two feet. He wove into his story students in our class, our teacher, and our principal. When he took the storytelling stool, he sat up straight, his eyes sparkled, and the class leaned forward in anticipation.

Listening to this fourth-grade master at work, I dreamt of captivating the class (nay, the school!) the way he did. But try as I might, my writing was just a ten-year-old's blurry copy of Tolkien's world. As I climbed the stool and read my unimaginative retelling of *The Hobbit*, I watched my class-mates' shoulders drop and caught glimpses of yawns over the top of my cursive-filled pages.

My competing fourth-grade author had figured out some-thing I hadn't yet: how to write for an audience. His secret sauce was writing with the listener in mind. I wrote for the anticipated accolades.

Write for the Audience You Already Have

Why are you considering blogging? Who do you hope will read what you write? You need crystal clear answers to those two questions.

I often listen to Jeff Brown's podcast *Read to Lead*. It's an interview-style podcast where Brown hosts authors and speakers. At the end of the podcast he asks the same set of questions to each interviewee, including "What tips do you have to give an impactful speech?" One of the most common responses to that question is an encouragement for the speaker to get to know his or her audience. Multiple authors have said the same thing: "get to the conference early," "sit down over coffee with other attendees," and "be present." It's great advice and no less true for an author than a speaker.

The most successful authors know their audiences. Read-ers who feel known become invested and loyal. Readers who feel like a number become disinterested and flighty.

So, who is your audience?

When I ask that question, I want you to think of real peo-ple you know, friends and family. Don't leap to an imaginary audience before you deal with the readers you actually know. Who are the first two dozen people who will subscribe to your blog? What do they have in common? What interests, beliefs, and hobbies do they share? In Seth Godin's book *Tribes* he defines a tribe as "a group of people connected to one another, connected to a leader, and connected to an idea."[1] The three legs of Godin's stool are very helpful for discerning your readership: define the group, understand yourself as a leader, and define the idea to which you will continue circling back. Learn these characteristics of your audience, and craft posts for them.

My first audience is my congregation. I serve as a co-lead pastor at New Life Bible Fellowship in Tucson, Arizona. I write as a ministry for the local church God has called me to serve.

> I would love to see more pastors blogging. Even if a new pastor blogger does not ever gain widespread readership, he can almost certainly know that his congregation will follow and read his blog. – David Qaoud, *gospelrelevance.com*

The first church I pastored was in New Jersey in the same town as the seminary I attended. Two professors who instructed me in seminary now sat under my preaching. They were godly men whose understanding of Scripture far exceeded my own. My stomach twisted in knots as I thought about standing in front of these men whose approval I desired. So I envisioned them as the audience of my first sermons and worked hard to make them proud. That was a mistake. They were far from representative of the congregation God had called me to shepherd. Bloggers can make an equivalent mistake. Don't write your blog for your favorite authors or public figures; write it for those who will be your first cadre of readers.

---

[1] Seth Godin, *Tribes: We Need You to Lead Us* (New York: Penguin, 2008), 1.

Once you have your *who* established, you can begin to shape your *why*. The two are connected. You can have a powerful *why*, but if that *why* doesn't connect with your *who*, your blog will fall flat.

There is an internationally known author who has challenged and helped me develop my theology in many ways. However, he often seems to misunderstand his audience. This extremely sharp author appeals to an educated Christian audience, yet one of his hobbyhorses is bashing a type of paper-thin Christianity that believes faith is merely punching one's ticket to heaven. His critique rings true enough, but I doubt many in his audience are guilty of this theological crime.

I recently heard this author on a podcast lambast this type of Christianity. It was clear that he was trying to convince his audience that this wasn't what Christianity was about, that Christianity was living the life of Christ in the context of one's community. He went on and on about all of these Christians who thought Christianity was just about getting to heaven, about how these Christians were neglecting the heart of the Christian calling, and how the New Testament shows us a very different type of Christianity. I scratched my head, "Who is he talking to?" I don't rub shoulders with the type of Christian he is talking about, and I certainly doubt that type of Christian is listening to this podcast.

The host of the podcast then directed the conversation toward the difficult topic of how Christians should respond to the issue of homosexuality. It's a topic that I'm certain this author's audience has a wide range of views on and a topic on which this author is particularly well suited to provide wisdom and direction. In fact, the author said he had devoted countless hours of study to the topic and "has a whole bookshelf of books on the subject." But he dodged the question, refusing to provide any wisdom on a timely subject that mattered deeply to his audience, though he was uniquely equipped to answer. As soon as the host asked the question, I'm sure listeners everywhere turned up their iPhones and stopped multitasking only to be disappointed.

> Blogging is an especially good platform for apologetics. Living in a multi-ethnic and multi-religious country, we need sharp, trained, intelligent bloggers online defending the faith. – *Tom Terry*, *tomthinking.com*

This author, as brilliant as he is, misunderstood his audience. For an hour he spoke past his audience to an imaginary one and then refused to engage an issue that would have actually mattered to his listeners.

Don't ignore your true audience for the audience you want, however noble your desire is to engage that imaginary audience "out there." Your blog isn't the field of dreams. "If you build it, they will come" is unlikely to work with your blog. Build your blog for those who are already there. Serve them.

What's Your White-Hot Why?

If you're reading this book, you have a passion to make a difference with your words. What difference do you want to make? That is your *why*.

Do you want to encourage moms of young children? Offer tools for Christians to grow in stewardship? Help Christians make wise choices with media? Inspire other Christian artists to create art that glorifies God? All worthy goals.

Connect that *why* to your *who* and you have a powerful tool for real change.

Why do I blog? Under the authority of the Great Shepherd, I blog as an extension of my call to faithfully shepherd God's people at New Life Bible Fellowship. I blog as a way to extend my discipleship of God's people through exhortation and encouragement. What's my *why*? Shepherding. And my *who* is the people of New Life Bible Fellowship.

What is your *why*? How does that connect to your *who*?

One reason this exercise is so important is that it can help protect you from selfish motives in blogging. If we are to blog in a way that honors God, we must demonstrate the character of Christ in doing so. A quick scan of the "how-to" literature on blogging reveals two primary motives for blogging:

1) to build one's platform, and

2) to make money.

While it is possible that blogging can serve to build your platform or perhaps earn you money, if either one of those is your chief *why*, then what you are doing is not likely to glorify God. If your blog is to honor God, it must serve others first, not yourself. I love Kevin DeYoung's honesty when he reflects on his ministry. He looks at his own heart and says, "Do I want money and recognition? Do I feel the need for validation? Do I like it when I look successful? Or do I want people to learn more about Christ and honor him with their lives? Yes, yes, yes, and yes. I pray that my heart is mostly concerned with the last yes, but sometimes it's hard to tell."[2]

---

[2] Kevin DeYoung, "The Fetid Pool," *The Gospel Coalition*, January 27, 2010, https://www.thegospelcoalition.org/blogs/kevin-deyoung/the-fetid-pool/.

My heart is a swirl of affections and desires. What does it look like for me to fan the flame of the most God-glorifying desires of my heart?

I was late to blogging. I toyed with the idea of blogging years before I began. If you would have asked me a decade ago why I was considering blogging, I believe I would have answered along these lines: "To extend my shepherding ministry to a broader audience." By "broader audience," I mostly meant building my platform.

Fortunately, I felt sufficiently uneasy about my motives and held off. I'm glad I did. What eventually compelled me to begin my blog wasn't a desire to increase my platform but to deepen my shepherding influence on the people of New Life beyond Sunday morning. I felt that one of the best ways I could serve New Life was through my writing.

> I wish when I had started blogging I had been more settled in my own voice. On reflection, my writing was far too reactive—feeding off the stimuli around me, I continually chased after "leads" and focused on responding to issues. I wish I had known to simply major on the gospel. – *Chris Thomas*, *ploughmansrest.com*

Before I began my blog I thought long and hard about whom I wanted to reach. I knew God had given me the gift of writing, and so I felt that at this stage of my life I needed to steward that gift better. But most of the bloggers I followed wrote for large, national audiences. While the thought of writing for a large audience was attractive, I realized the audience "out there" was disconnected from my primary pastoral call to my local congregation.

As I began to reflect more on my pastoral ministry, I realized that my audience wasn't some mythical group of people "out there." Rather, it was the congregation I served week in, week out. The gift of writing for this group is that I know them. I know their passions, and I know their struggles. I also believed that in a world where we get roughly thirty-five minutes a week (for the super-faithful, weekly attenders) to speak God's truth into their lives, having another venue to pastor them would be invaluable.

This became my white-hot *why*—deepening the discipleship of God's people at New Life. If my blog reaches others beyond New Life that is great, but my first audience will always be the people God called me to in Tucson.

Why Paul Offered Himself to Corinth for Jesus's Sake

Of all the churches Paul ministered to, the church at Corinth might have been the most difficult. They were bull-headed and rebellious. Despite how difficult they were to love, Paul explains his aim in 2 Corinthians 1:24, "we work with you for your joy, for you stand firm in your faith." Everything Paul writes in 2 Corinthians is for the sake of helping the church at Corinth to stand firm in their faith.

No matter what type of blog you're writing, your blog is a very personal endeavor. You can't write without being personal. So, as you begin to consider what type of blog God is calling you to write, also consider who you are and what God is doing in your life.

As with any endeavor, if your blog isn't authentic to you, over time your audience will sniff it out. And if it's not authentic, you have little chance of doing the hard work of grinding out material and developing and maintaining a consistent, trustworthy voice.

Paul shares in 2 Corinthians that his desire isn't to shine the light on himself. He wants the light of Christ to shine into the hearts of the Corinthians. In 2 Corinthians 4:5, he says, "For what we proclaim is not ourselves, but Jesus Christ as Lord, with ourselves as your servants for Jesus' sake."

You might be surprised, then, that Paul shares as much about himself as he does in 2 Corinthians. If Paul's purpose isn't to proclaim himself, but Jesus Christ, one might assume that Paul wouldn't share about himself. But that isn't the case at all; in fact, 2 Corinthians is Paul's most autobiographical letter. He shares much of his own story not because he is narcissistic but because he knows the church is struggling to trust him and he needs to build rapport.

Where can you offer yourself to your audience for the sake of proclaiming Jesus Christ as Lord? How can your life become a bridge for the gospel to travel? What work has God done (or is doing) in you that will encourage others?

Shaping Your Call

One of the most disconcerting trends of many books on blogging is the encouragement for authors to go after trendy and bankable topics (most of these types of books include the words "for profit" in the title). Don't fall into this trap. Don't feel compelled to chase whatever is hot. Be true to who God has made you to be. Paul flips our impulse on its head: "I will most gladly spend and be spent for your souls" (2 Cor 12:14). Don't use your audience. Be spent for them.

Here are some questions that might help you discern the voice God has given you to minister to the audience he has given you.

- If no one ever reads your writing, what do you hope to achieve? How do you want the habit of blogging to form you? How do you want your commitment to blogging to shape your character?

- How has God worked in your life? How is he working in your life today?
- How much are you willing to disclose in your writing? How much is appropriate to disclose? Are there those near you whom you will need to ask for permission to share parts of your story?
- What is your passion for the church? How are you serving the church today?
- What has God taught you about himself that you want every person you meet to know about?
- Imagine two years from now: you query your faithful readers to describe your blog in one sentence. What do you hope they would say? What do you want your primary benefit to your audience to be?

When I began my blog I didn't know how many people would read it. But I felt compelled that failing to steward the gift of writing God had given me to disciple his people would be disobedient. Even if I was writing just for a handful of people, faithfulness to God meant writing faithfully to his people.

Chasing Your Call, Not the News Cycle

Understanding your *why* and your *who* also helps you know what *not* to write about. When I know why I'm writing and whom I'm writing for, all sorts of topics fall off the table. I'm a huge sports fan and a particularly nerdy baseball fan. I've written drafts of posts introducing casual fans to concepts like Wins Above Replacement, WHIP, and ERA+. I've actually written drafts where I have projected the expected regression of teams based on their run differential. (If you have no idea what I'm talking about, congratulations, you are much cooler than me.) I've written posts dissecting the changing political landscape. I've written posts on theological minutiae. And no part of any of these posts has seen the light of day. I'm sure my audience remains grateful for that, both because I'm not an expert in any of those fields and because my audience (in general) doesn't really care about those areas or about my opinion on those matters.

I've read plenty of posts on topics that I do know a fair bit about (the Bible, the church, etc.) from those who don't have in-depth knowledge of what they're talking about. Such posts only hurt the author's credibility. Don't go out of your depth in areas where you're not a strong swimmer. Do you need to be an expert to talk about something? No. But do you need to know more than the average person and do some decent fact-checking? Absolutely.

Perhaps the biggest lure to any blogger is the power of the 24-hour news cycle. Many blogs are held captive to the latest comings-and-goings of the world of headlines. It feels fresh to engage the topics of the day. People are more likely to click on your headline to read your take. It can provide you opportunities that you wouldn't have otherwise.

Many years ago news concerning Tiger Woods's infidelity captured the public's eye. I posted a reflection on his demise on a friend's site and it blew up (by my modest standards). It was exciting to see the number of readers spike for the blog and see it shared fairly widely. It was a great dopamine hit. I could keep going after that hit. I could write about a new scandal every week. But I've realized over time that responding to the news cycle rarely fits with my purpose and audience.

Why not? Because I primarily want to write posts that have an evergreen quality. I want to write posts that can be read a few years later and still be meaningful to the reader. Second, while engaging culture, I want to provide a voice different than the news cycle, which can so quickly pull us in its undertow. Third, I want to follow, to the best of my ability, Paul's admonition to think upon that which is pure, lovely, and commendable (Phil 4:8). If I can put that in business terms, I want my brand to be about building up, not tearing down. The reality is that the vast majority of articles bound to the news cycle lend themselves to tearing down. I know my own nature is to tend toward cynicism and biting sarcasm. Another early post I wrote basically tore to shreds children's and toddlers' Bibles on the market. I wish I had never published the article. Are there things that deserve criticism? Certainly. Do I want to make sure that I'm judicious about when I choose to be critical? Most certainly.

> One of the most difficult things about blogging is finding worthwhile topics to write about regularly. Too many bloggers, including me, get caught up in writing about current events or whatever everyone else is talking about at the moment. If you do that long enough, you realize you've mostly just wasted your time (and everyone else's too). – *Joe Carter, <u>thegospelcoalition.org</u>*

While such trend-worthy stories can provide some tinder for your fire, they are a poor substitute for the substantial logs that give off the warmth your readers need.

God may be calling you to write in a way that addresses the issues of the day. My point isn't to criticize those who do. I think of Russell Moore and Joe Carter as examples of those who respond in a wise and grace-filled manner to the news cycle. But, my perception is that too many bloggers rely on the news cycle to generate interest. It only takes a day on Twitter to realize there are far too many who feel compelled to offer their opinion on every scrap of news that hits the internet.

Having a strong *why* and *who* doesn't mean every post will look the same. Creative communicators realize the need for different approaches to drive their message home and to keep their audience engaged.

A Balanced Meal

In their book *Content Rules*, authors Ann Handley and C. C. Chapman liken this to a meal.[3] You need to serve your audience a varied meal. Dan Carlin's podcast on history is excellent, but every episode is roughly three to four hours long and every topic spans several podcasts. A very niche audience will slog through five three-hour podcasts on the Gaelic Wars. All Carlin serves is steak. Steak is great, but it's unlikely that you'll be able to create a successful blog with just steak. I know a handful of great bloggers out there who only serve steak, but I have to carve out just the right time to be able to read their meaty blog posts. You want your audience to know you are going to offer substance while also being relatable. Don't be afraid to smile when you write.

On the flip side, you don't want to serve up popcorn and soda for every post. Popcorn, candy, and soda are great accompaniments to a movie, but if the trio has become the staple of your diet, you're in trouble. Feel free to include fun, even clickbait-y, posts from time to time. You don't have to

[3] Ann Handley and C. C. Chapman, *Content Rules: How to Create Killer Blogs, Podcasts, Videos, Ebooks, Webinars (and More) That Engage Customers and Ignite Your Business* (Hoboken, New Jersey: John Wiley & Sons, 2012), 245–47.

take yourself too seriously. But serve up hearty meals on a regular basis to go along with the popcorn and candy. I don't necessarily mean intellectually heavy, but I do mean something substantive, something that moves your audience toward the heart of Christ.

God has gifted you with a unique personality, calling, and audience. How are you going to steward those for his glory? Where is the intersection of your *why* and *who*? Dig your shovel into this soil that God has given you to garden.

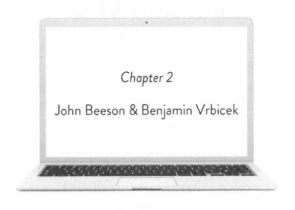

Chapter 2

John Beeson & Benjamin Vrbicek

DISCIPLINES

How Do I Spiritually Grow While Blogging?

I was told not to equate preparing for sermons with devotional Bible reading. There is truth in that encouragement. If we professionalize spiritual disciplines, then our spiritual life tends to become stuffy and transactional from expecting that clocking in yields certain results. On the other hand, I've learned if the posture of my heart in my sermon preparation isn't devotional, then my preaching becomes dry and academic. If I am not growing spiritually through my pastoral ministry, I'm not pastoring as God intended. I would say the same thing to engineers, teachers, stay-at-home moms, and salespeople. I'd say the same thing to bloggers.[1]

Blogging ought to grow us in holiness. When we blog for God's glory, the discipline of writing becomes integrated into the web of our spiritual disciplines. In this chapter we'll explore how blogging can be cultivated as a companion to

---

[1] The first half of this chapter was written by John and the last half by Benjamin.

spiritual disciplines and even as a spiritual discipline in its own right. Before we consider this, we want to send up a warning flare: challenges for the Christian blogger abound.

We are writing this chapter in the heart of the COVID-19 outbreak. Anyone who thought the news cycle was fast before could never have predicted what 2020 would bring. It's not just the speed of the news that is alarming; it's the demand for a response. Woke culture requires we weigh in on every injustice lest we are complicit in evil, and call-out culture requires anger without grace.

Our mediums of public communication compound the problem. Twitter and Facebook are immediate, unfiltered, and democratized. As bloggers, we can feel the pressure to respond. That impulse may be appropriate, but we must remember that the work required to produce balance, nuance, and truth is far greater than what it takes to post falsehood and distortion. Moreover, our impulse to write can arise out of anger, arrogance, and self-interest, along with the desire to score pageviews off a cultural moment.

Writing is always fraught with significant challenges in the pursuit of holiness, but avoiding danger seems to require more vigilance when culture scatters sticky traps around every issue. In this day, how can our blogging cultivate the fruit of the Spirit rather than the fruit of the flesh?

In his book *Habits of Grace*, David Mathis suggests there are three basic forms of spiritual disciplines: hearing God's voice through the Bible, having God's ear through prayer, and belonging to God's body through Christian fellowship.[2] Let's consider a blogger's cultivation of Christian character through these three clusters of spiritual disciplines.

---

[2] David Mathis, *Habits of Grace: Enjoying Jesus through the Spiritual Disciplines* (Wheaton: Crossway, 2016).

Hearing God's Voice

If we are to speak for God, we need to hear from him. We need his encouragement, his exhortation, and his direction. Thankfully, he's the God who speaks. "For the LORD gives wisdom; from his mouth come knowledge and understanding" (Prov 2:6).

When Satan tempts Jesus to create bread after forty days of fasting in the wilderness, Jesus tells the enemy that even while he is starving, God's word is more essential than food. Quoting Deuteronomy 8:3, Jesus says, "Man shall not live by bread alone, but by every word that comes from the mouth of God" (Matt 4:4).

God can speak through various means, but he

> Christian blogs should be distinctive for their demonstration of humility and caution when publishing words online. We believe words have power. God spoke creation into existence, and he chose to reveal himself through Christ, which is given to us in the testimony of his disciples' words. Writing is sacred. – *Chase Replogle*, *chasereplogle.com*

speaks most clearly through his word. You probably have a hunger to write, but do you have a voracious appetite to consume God's word? If we have any hope of offering others wisdom, listening to God must become a primary and ongoing habit. Our human understanding is like the grass that withers and fades, while God's wisdom stands forever (Isa 40:8). Our writing is fallible; God's is infallible. Our writing is errant; his is inerrant. The world judges authors by their creativity and brilliance. But we know our words, no matter how pretty, will return to dust unless they convey God's truth.

This does not mean blogging that exposits Scripture is the only kind that glorifies God. But it does mean our writing, whether fiction, memoir, didactic, or some other style employed while covering topics not explicitly related to the Bible, is still subject to God's truth and ought to reflect his light. Around forty authors on three continents across fifteen hundred years wrote the sixty-six books of the Bible. The authors came from all kinds of backgrounds and wrote in all sorts of styles. They wrote poetry, history, songs, wisdom, letters, and polemics. Incredibly—and in contrast to most holy books in other religions—each author's voice is distinct. The biblical authors were carried along by the Holy Spirit, but as the Holy Spirit directed them, their personalities remained wholly present.

This diversity of each author's personality and gifting should encourage us. We, of course, will never author Holy Scripture. But isn't it encouraging to know that even today God still delights in using an author's unique personality and situation, through the power of his Spirit, for his good work? It is not the size of our platform that assures us how far our words will reach, but rather it is our trust in a God whose word never returns void (Isa 55:11).

Having God's Ear

The Creator of the universe doesn't merely allow us to speak to him; he invites us to speak to him; he longs for us to talk to him. Because Jesus Christ put on flesh and entered our broken world, we know that we do not pray to a distant God. We converse with one who understands our pain and predicaments. "For we do not have a high priest who is unable to sympathize with our weaknesses," the author of Hebrews reminds us, "but one who in every respect has been tempted as we are, yet without sin." The exhortation that flows from this truth is that we should "with confidence draw near to the throne of grace, that we may receive mercy and find grace to help in time of need" (Heb 4:15–16). We must heed God's voice, but what an unexpected and wonderful truth that God would care to listen to ours.

As writers, prayer is essential not only in developing our inner character but also in shaping our output. In Colossians 4:2–4 Paul says it is through prayer that he aligns himself with God's motivations and intentions. "Continue steadfastly in prayer, being watchful in it with thanksgiving. At the same time, pray also for us, that God may open to us a door for the word, to declare the mystery of Christ, on account of which I am in prison—that I may make it clear, which is how I ought to speak."

Let me unpack this rich passage. Paul tells us that our prayer ought to be steadfast, watchful, and characterized by a grateful heart. A healthy prayer life is consistent and persistent. We pray when we rise in the morning, when we eat, and as we drift off to sleep. When we pray, we do so watchfully. We pray as those on the lookout for God's blessing, for the spiritual attacks against ourselves and others, for the advancement of God's kingdom, and for Christ's glorious return. And we pray with gratitude, as those with hearts full of thanksgiving.

These same attributes—steadfastness, watchfulness, and gratefulness—should also characterize our writing. The more we pray, the more our hearts will be shaped by steadfastness, watchfulness, and gratitude. And the more our hearts are characterized by these God-glorifying attributes, the more our writing will reflect him.

Notice, as well, the beautiful request Paul makes to his readers. "Pray also for us, that God may open to us a door for the word to declare the mystery of Christ, on account of which I am in prison—that I may make it clear, which is how I ought to speak." Paul shares such intimacy with his readers that he freely asks them for prayer, indeed a prayer asking that he be enabled to "declare the mystery of Christ" clearly.

Cultivating this kind of prayer life runs contrary to the impulse of our flesh. Blogging—even Christian blogging—tends to be directed by the cultural winds whirling around us. That current issue under a blogger's skin, that fuel feeding the brightest dumpster fire, that volley of words bouncing around our echo chamber—these all conspire to shape us more than our prayers. Don't let them.

Belonging to God's Body

In our individualized world, we tend to think of spiritual disciplines as something between God and us, but our pilgrimage toward Christlikeness is not a road traveled alone. God intends for us to live in community and under authority.

Let's return to Paul's letter to the church at Colossae to see what else he has to say about community.

> Put on then, as God's chosen ones, holy and beloved, compassionate hearts, kindness, humility, meekness, and patience, bearing with one another and, if one has a complaint against another, forgiving each other; as the Lord has forgiven you, so you also must forgive. And above all these put on love, which binds everything together in perfect harmony. And let the peace of Christ rule in your hearts, to which indeed you were called in one body. And be thankful. Let the word of Christ dwell in you richly, teaching and admonishing one another in

all wisdom, singing psalms and hymns and spiritual songs, with thankfulness in your hearts to God. And whatever you do, in word or deed, do everything in the name of the Lord Jesus, giving thanks to God the Father through him. (Col 3:12–17)

Paul's encouragement to participate in God's family requires more than superficial acknowledgment of God's family. Community is the gym where we exercise compassion, kindness, humility, forgiveness, and love. Paul's vision of community isn't whitewashed; he knows exactly how demanding it is to live with one another. Think what these admonitions imply. Our community *will* challenge us. We'll have to exercise compassion to the stone-hearted, kindness to the rude, humility to the proud, and forgiveness to those who wrong us. All of this will be for their spiritual benefit *and* ours. It's in God's community that we admonish one another, we sing praises to God, and we offer thanksgiving back to God. Thankfulness appears to be at the forefront of Paul's mind, as he mentions it three times in this paragraph about God's family.

Would you characterize your response to church as thankful? How do you feel the night before your small group Bible study? What goes through your mind on Sunday morning when you have to choose whether to stay in your pajamas with that hot cup of coffee or expend the energy to wrangle your family and head to church? In Glenna Marshall's book *Everyday Faithfulness,* she reminds us that "your church is God's gift to you."[3] If *your church is God's gift to you*, then you must have a local church to call yours. This is true

---

[3] Glenna Marshall, *Everyday Faithfulness: The Beauty of Ordinary Perseverance in a Demanding World* (Wheaton: Crossway, 2020), 108.

for all Christians but needs to be received just as warmly by bloggers who often have a network of online relationships that can (wrongly) become a substitute for their local church. Don't bypass your local church; it's there that God intends for you to find brothers and sisters who will encourage you to persevere when you are weary and will exhort you when your blog becomes cynical or self-serving.

We encourage you to reach out to your pastor and ask him to pray for you and hold you accountable. Pastors who blog have to submit to this same kind of accountability—or at least they should. It's a blessing to have pastor-elders who read our blogs, providing advice and accountability for our writing ministry.

Writing to glorify God means that we honor his bride, the church. If you are considering writing about someone in your church, critiquing your leadership, or expressing disappointment, we urge you to follow biblical principles of peacemaking (see Jesus's admonition in Matt 18:15, "If your brother sins against you, go and tell him his fault, between you and him alone."). One of the common tropes of Christian blogging expresses concern that the church isn't paying enough attention to a given issue, whether that's racism, abortion, pornography, singleness, or something else. Before you write that post, consider reaching out to your pastor. Maybe he has a blind spot; or perhaps you do. Venting to a listening world can feel courageous, but the harder move, the one that requires faith and the one that

> Every blogger should speak under the authority of proper local church leadership. Too many have built a following to speak authoritatively without sound theological training, wisdom, and humility. Writers should be working in conjunction with a local church and elders.
> – Jeremy Writebol, *jwritebol.net*

God desires you to make first, involves going to your brothers and sisters before you go to the blogosphere. This may be more difficult, but it's the system God designed for his glory and our good.

The Spiritual Disciplines Produce Discernment

King Solomon reminds us of the danger of unfiltered speech when he says, "A fool gives full vent to his spirit, but a wise man quietly holds it back" (Prov 29:11). Godly and wise writing—that is, writing as an overflow of a life vitally connected to God through the spiritual disciplines—results in growing spiritual discernment. This is true both for the craft itself and in the posture of our hearts.

In her book *The Writing Life*, Annie Dillard describes writing as making several thousand close judgment calls.[4] William Zinsser concurs in his famous book *On Writing Well*: "Professional writers rewrite their sentences over and over and then rewrite what they have rewritten."[5]

Dillard and Zinsser have in mind the thousand literary micro-decisions involved in perfecting a piece of prose, including the choices of diction, syntax, pace, tone, concision, punctuation, and whether adding a pinch of verbal cayenne pepper would spice up the sentence or overwhelm it.

All of these choices require discernment on the part of the practitioner, like a visit to an eye doctor who repeatedly interrogates whether *this one* looks better or *this one* does. "Again," the eye doctor asks, "this one or this one? Okay, now, this or this? This or this?"

---

[4] Annie Dillard, *The Writing Life* (New York: Harper Perennial, 2013), 11.
[5] William Zinsser, *On Writing Well, 30th Anniversary Edition: An Informal Guide to Writing Nonfiction* (New York: Harper Perennial, 2006), 4.

Writing comes down to making and remaking slight improvements to achieve better clarity and aesthetic; writing is the pursuit of marginal gains, insignificant by themselves but significant in the aggregate. Do I break this paragraph here or there? Do I tell a story to begin a chapter or favor a provocative propositional statement? Should I insert dialogue, and if so, do I use direct or indirect? And if an editor has suggested I write some sentence or other in the active voice rather than letting the sentence be written in the passive, which shall I choose? Could the sentence in question be a place where the passive voice is actually better?

All of a sudden you realize that the passing line from Dillard about writing involving several thousand close judgment calls might not be hyperbole. Writers must love these choices and labor to make them better. "Rewriting," says Zinsser, "is the essence of writing."[6]

So, if Dillard and Zinsser can exhort a general audience to care about their lines of words so much, how much more shall we, those redeemed by the Word made flesh, care about the beauty of our prose? Christians called by God to write must strive to write well. We would argue that the craft of writing itself is a spiritual discipline.

Adorning Truth

But beautiful language, by itself, does not encompass all that it means to write well as a Christian. Christian writers must labor not only to write what is true but also to write in a manner that adorns the truth. For example, I love my wife, but if I shout, "I love you"—a true statement—with my nose tip touching her nose in the dark at 5:00 a.m., she won't feel

[6] Ibid.

loved. Can you blame her? She'll feel loved when, after she wakes up and has her Diet Coke, I hold both her hands in mine, look her in the eyes, and surprise her with news that I got a babysitter and movie tickets.

These two aspects of Christian writing—writing truth and writing that adorns the truth—are often missing in writing on the internet. In a post about the aim of Christian writing, Cody Cunningham notes that "too many Christian blogs—often self-identified as 'truth-tellers'—are merely cheap imitations of American culture's response du jour: outrage and snark."[7] There are consequences of this cultural discipleship among Christian writers, not the least of which is God's name being blasphemed among the Gentiles on account of those who claim to be writing on God's behalf.

The pervasiveness of sinful speech on the internet is so bad, it can cause some Christians to wonder if it would be better if we abandoned it altogether because the medium is too tainted. Brett McCracken has even called the internet a "cesspool of spiritual bacteria," understanding the temptation to flee to the "analog hills."[8] But a better approach, he argues, would be to redeem rather than abandon. McCracken writes, "like the leper colonies, Ebola-stricken nations, or plague-infested medieval cities where Christians risked their own health to bring healing to others, the internet desperately needs people of light to stay rather than to leave."[9] But if we do stay—and we *do* want you to stay if you're already blogging and to get in the game if you're on the sidelines—then we must possess discernment.

---

[7] Cody Cunningham, "The Aim of Christian Writing," *CodyCunningham.com*, July 24, 2020, https://codyacunningham.com/2019/07/24/what-is-the-aim-of-christian-writing/.

[8] Brett McCracken, "The Digital Revolution Reformation," *The Gospel Coalition*, November 19, 2019, https://www.thegospelcoalition.org/article/digital-revolution-reformation/.

[9] Ibid.

Exposing Darkness

Paul writes in Ephesians that we must take "no part in the unfruitful works of darkness, but instead expose them. For it is shameful even to speak of the things that they do in secret" (Eph 5:11–12). Do you see the tension in these verses? On the one hand, expose. On the other hand, even speaking about certain sins is shameful. Resolving this tension requires discernment. Without the cultivation of discernment, we'll be sucked into the cesspool without even realizing it. This is true for any Christian writer, but especially those so-called discernment bloggers who major in exposing sin, sinners, and theological error.

Is it possible you might need to courageously expose sin or theological error at some point as a blogger? Yes. Is it likely a God-glorifying blog is marked by a critical tone? No.

Too many self-proclaimed discernment bloggers do not have the spiritual gift of discernment, nor meaningful membership in a local church for that matter, which should keep a blogger grounded and accountable. To be clear, bloggers are not obliged to meet the requirements for eldership listed in 1 Timothy 3:1–7 and 1 Peter 5:1–4. But shouldn't we aspire to do so? Shouldn't we aspire to be "sober-minded, self-controlled, respectable, hospitable, able to teach, . . . not violent but gentle, not quarrelsome"? Shouldn't we strive not to be "domineering over those in [our] charge" but rather the kinds of examples that the Chief Shepherd will reward when he appears and bestows "the unfading crown of glory"? We should. In the Bible, godly prophets loved the people they chastised. And they still do today.

Furthermore, such a relationship with the local church and submission to her leaders will help set a Christian blogger's sights on building up God's people. This mission is set in stark relief to getting views by tearing down others.

A few months ago a friend at church sent me a text message about an article he read. The title of the post was "Lesbian Feminist Receives The Gospel Coalition's 2019 Book Award for Evangelism and Apologetics." The author, showing no discernment, titled his article this way even though the female author of the book is in a committed, heterosexual marriage, which I'm quite sure is not the definition of a lesbian. At the time I clicked the bait, the article had been shared on Facebook three thousand more times than any article I have ever written. The whole piece was smeared with unsubstantiated slander. This makes the article (and the particular website, for that matter) an extreme example. But it's often in the extreme that we see the principle: "A fool takes no pleasure in understanding, but only in expressing his opinion" (Prov 18:2).

> Bloggers should "preach" under the authority of their local church and pastor. Bloggers are teachers and need accountability. Their own local church is the best place to get that. – *Melissa Edgington, yourmomhasablog.com*

Let's press in a bit further by asking hard questions. How does one discern the credibility of an allegation? And how do readers know if a blogger has the expertise and education and the backing of a reputable organization to verify the credibility of an allegation over and against mere gossip and opinion? And perhaps more to the point of our book—how does a blogger know if he or she has the ability to verify allegations? We're not raising these questions to discount the good work done by many bloggers on behalf of victims of abuse, especially abuse within particular churches. Praise God when truth comes to light. In the light, people can heal and justice can reign. But many internet armchair investigators have neither the education nor the peer-reviewed scrutiny that has produced the reporting of, say, Julie Roys on Harvest Church in World Magazine or the *Houston Chronicle* exposing sexual scandals in the Southern Baptist Convention.[10] The Disney movie *Ratatouille* had that great line, "anyone can cook," just as we suppose anyone can blog. Let's not compare, however, the food prepared in a restaurant that earns Michelin Stars to serving mac 'n cheese with chopped hot dogs.

In a day when *sick burns* get more clicks than a gentle, loving rebuke, why should we bother being measured in our approach? A brief perusal of YouTube demonstrates just how many sell their wares with the promise of a burn. So why should we worry about getting the tone and the content right when we know fewer people will read an article if we write with discernment? We bother because God is God, and on the day of judgment we will give an account for every careless word we have ever blogged (Matt 12:36). In the section of his epistle on our inability to tame our tongue, James writes that not many should become teachers, for we will be judged more strictly (3:1). In the same way, not many of us should become bloggers, let alone discernment bloggers.

But some of us should take up this role, just as some of us are called by God to be teachers. For those who are, you must labor to cultivate the gift you claim to have. Pursue discernment for the sake of God's honor, the edification of others, and your own eternal joy—even if you get fewer clicks.

---

[10] Julie Roys, "Hard times at Harvest," *World Magazine*, December 13, 2018, https://world.wng.org/2018/12/hard_times_at_harvest, and. Robert Downen, Lise Olsen, and John Tedesco, "Abuse of Faith," *Houston Chronicle*, February 10, 2019, https://www.houstonchronicle.com/news/investigations/article/Southern-Baptist-sexual-abuse-spreads-as-leaders-13588038.php.

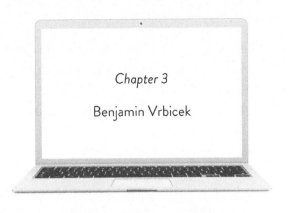

Chapter 3

Benjamin Vrbicek

COMMITMENT

How Much Time and Effort Will Blogging Take?

I published my first blog post on July 22, nearly seven years ago, with the title "Fresh Words, Fresh Language, Fresh Blood." In the post I discussed two different ways we can lose the historic message of Christianity. First, we can simply stop communicating the message of Christianity. When we disconnect the power to live the Christian life from the message of Christianity, that is, the once-for-all-delivered gospel—the life, death, resurrection, ascension, and second coming of Jesus—Christianity becomes meaningless and powerless. This, I said in the post, was the death of severing arteries from the heart: you can't live long without lifeblood pumping from the source.

But there is a second way to anesthetize Christianity, I argued. We can use stale, tired, and jargon-filled language to preach the message of Christianity. This is a slower death, one of recirculating oxygen-depleted blood. For example, a blogger could encourage a reader to "invite Jesus into her heart," but what does this phrase even mean? Overuse has made the phrase meaningless.

As I look back on my first blog post, it reads a wee bit sophomoric. I'm not as clever as I thought. But I made these points in my first post because I hoped my blog would offer readers the historic message of Christian hope with fresh words, fresh language, fresh blood—not stale, rehearsed, clichéd language. I prayed God would use my blog to fan into flame joy in the gospel as I tried my best to share the once-for-all-delivered message of Christianity with accessible and riveting language. I wanted to pump fresh, oxygen-rich blood into Christ's body. For that reason I called my blog "Fan and Flame."

In the post I interacted with an episode of a famous author's podcast. When I started blogging, I made the rule to always reach out to other authors when I interacted with their work on my blog. I encourage you to do this too. So I sent the famous author an email. He wrote back, which still surprises me. He thanked me for being a local church pastor, which is where, he said, real ministry lives. I remember getting his email almost more than publishing my first post.

I'm writing all of this to say that, a few hundred blog posts later, none are as memorable to me as my first; a tailwind blew me along as I ran downhill with a smile. Growing up I hated to read and write. I'd take calculus over an English class every time. But in those days of planning to launch a blog, God was changing my passions in life. And I loved it.

A few blog posts later, my family and I were headed on vacation to visit relatives. We stopped at a hotel somewhere in Indiana because we didn't make it far enough. Too many miles, too many kids stopping for potty breaks, and probably too many repeats of "Are we there yet?" slowed us down. After the kids went to bed, I walked to the bathroom, turned on the light, sat on the edge of the bathtub, plugged in my laptop, opened it up, and started to tinker with another post. I still felt the wind at my back, but the breeze didn't seem to blow quite as strong. I still had a smile in my heart, but I also knew I probably should have posted two days earlier.

It was only my third post, and already I felt behind.

Our contention in this book is that glorifying God in our blogging means several things, but primarily it means having our motivations aligned with God's. Christians should not write for self-promotion. Let Jesus increase and authors decrease. Let his name be hallowed and ours be forgotten. Let the kingdom of Christ's love come and ours surrender. These are the motivations that propel Christians "further up and further in," to use Lewis's refrain in *The Last Battle*. The glory of God alone can sustain us bloggers when our traffic tanks and readers unsubscribe. It keeps us from the cynicism of Jack Black's character Dewey Finn in the movie *School of Rock*: "So don't waste your time trying to make anything cool, or pure, or awesome, 'cause the Man is just gonna call you a fat, washed-up loser and crush your soul. So do yourselves a favor and just give up!"[1] Too many long-abandoned Christian blogs are like gravestones marking crushed souls. It's so easy to be crushed with Dewey-Finn-like discouragement. If you're going to blog, we promise you at some point or another, you're going to hear Dewey's voice whispering, "Do yourself a favor and just give up!" And on the other end of the spectrum, the aim of magnifying God's name will keep you humble when Tim Challies serves up a

[1] Jack Black, *School of Rock*, DVD, directed by Richard Linklater (Los Angeles: Paramount Pictures, 2003).

link to your blog in his *A La Carte* email.

But blogging for God's glory means more than having the right motivations. In this chapter I want to explore how blogging for God's glory means evaluating all of the commitments God has placed in our life and how blogging, if we commit to it, relates to those other commitments. Blogging makes a great hobby but a terrible taskmaster; without really noticing, you can find yourself shut in a bathroom at midnight on vacation anxiously writing a post.

The Perfect Will of God

In the book of Romans, after spending eleven chapters expounding the height and depth and breadth of the gospel, the apostle Paul appeals by the mercy of God to live lives of joyful, obedient sacrifice. As those saved from wrath and now justified so that we experience joyful reconciliation with our Creator, we're called to be transformed, to renew our minds, and to discern the will of God. Paul says, "that by testing you may discern what is the will of God, what is good and acceptable and perfect" (Rom 12:2). The will of God is perfect; think about that.

Every so often, I'll accidentally schedule two events at the same time, one in my church calendar and another in my personal calendar. A few weeks ago I was supposed to officiate a Sunday afternoon wedding on the same day our church celebrated our twentieth anniversary. A picnic and five baptisms were planned. Obviously, I had made a big scheduling mistake; months and months before that Sunday I'd doubled-booked myself, though I only noticed it a few weeks beforehand. Typically, I'm a reasonably good planner, yet mistakes like this remind me that I'm far from perfect.

But God is a perfect planner, which means to obey the perfect will of God in one setting doesn't mean you necessarily disobey in another. We don't have to read our Bible and mow the grass and pick our kids up from the bus stop at the same time. By his design, we are finite creatures. Our finitude may frustrate our inner go-getter from time to time.

Just think how many to-do lists I could crush if I could be in two places at once. I could baptize people in a pond while wearing a suit and officiating a wedding. But our creaturely finitude, I assure you, doesn't bother God.

> A big mistake in blogging comes from writing from pressure. It produces "faithless writing," writing that's motivated by people's praise, approval, or attention, and not by the Lord and his Word. – *Kristen Wetherell*, *kristenwetherell.com*

When he saw everything he had made—which climaxed with the sculpting of a clump of dirt and a rib into two finite and non-omnipresent people—God called what he had made "very good" (Gen 1:31). Our finitude is good and so is the revealed will of God for us.

The perfect will of God encourages me when life feels out of control. I have six children to love and raise, a church to lead, exercise and hobbies to enjoy, and a calling—I believe from God—to write. And taking seriously the call to write means considering all that comes with it: a call to read, to build friendships with people who support your work, to develop relationships with editors, to invest in books and perhaps classes on writing, to become familiar with blogging platforms and email services, and so on. Thus the call to do one thing (to write) is a call to do many things. This, again, is why a vibrant faith in the perfect will of the Lord encourages me when my life seems too crazy to be livable. Jesus fulfilled many roles and faced many challenges during his earthly life, but as I read the Gospels I don't get the sense Jesus was flustered and hurried. Even the Son of God, in his humanity, did not sail the Sea of Galilee and preach in the temple grounds at the same time.

Consider Your Regular Blogging Rhythms

What does all this mean for your blogging? It means you need to consider your life patterns and your blogging patterns and how they relate to what God is calling you to do. On the one hand, if you are truly called to write, it's disobedient not to write. Too many aspiring writers start a blog but write with no perceivable pattern. They just sort of, you know, write when they feel time allows or when some idea strikes them as compelling. In other words, they never write. Maybe you already have a blog set up, but your last post was eighteen months ago. We understand. Life happens. We're glad you're reading. Hopefully our book can help nurse your excitement back to life.

Perhaps it's the other side of the spectrum where you struggle. You hear about bloggers posting each day, or even each weekday, and you try to do the same. *I'm only a blogger if I blogged today*, you think. Around the corner you sense burnout approaching—if it hasn't already arrived.

So let's consider different areas of your blog and how you'll approach each.

How much time will you give to blogging?

The first question to consider is how much time you plan to devote to blogging each week and when you will schedule this time. I'm sure a few bloggers spend thirty hours a week blogging because blogging has become a significant source of income. But the number of bloggers who receive any income, let alone anything that could be considered significant, are extremely few. Some hobbyists might spend fifteen hours blogging each week, but I assume that most do not. The size of your posts, whether 400-word quick reflections or 4,000-word long-form articles, will determine how much time you spend, as will the frequency of your posts. I have no statistics on this, but I'd

> Write a plan for your blog, put in the research, and seek to glorify God more than anything else. A plan helps you stay away from your hobbyhorses, it helps you build momentum with your posts, and it helps provide continuity for your readers. – *Alistair Chalmers, achalmersblog.com*

guess most active bloggers spend between two and ten hours per week, with the bulk of the bell curve near six hours. If you want to post two 800-word posts a week with one "round-up" type of post where you share articles from around the internet that will benefit your readers, you're looking at around eight to ten hours a week.

If I were shooting for that kind of output—the publishing of three articles a week—it would take me far longer. I'm a slow blogger. It takes me a long time to write and rewrite . . . and rewrite . . . and rewrite. Once a post is written, I'm pretty efficient at posting and setting up the email to my readers. Still, even with posts already written and edited, it takes me thirty minutes to publish on my website and schedule the email to my readers. That's why I only post once a week. If I did any more than this, I'd be neglecting the other responsibilities God has called me to steward.

I've tried to write one blog post a week for the last seven years, though I've never made it to fifty-two. Most years I make it to the mid-forties. The first year I didn't give as much time to blogging, but for the last six years I've spent about ten hours writing each week, with that time shared between blog posts for my site, guest posts for other sites, and book projects. I treat these ten hours like a part-time job.

When and where will you write?

Some people love to write in a coffee shop. Others prefer the silence of late nights or early mornings. Wherever you write, I'd encourage you to have a place you consistently work. And it is work. As some have said, art is more perspiration than inspiration.

I do most of my writing at our kitchen table every day (except Sunday) before our kids get up, so typically from 5:30–7:00 a.m. I don't work at church on Fridays, so during the school year I often get another ninety minutes in the afternoon to write while my younger kids nap and the older ones are at school. For me, plodding along in these small doses has been better than marathon binge writing. I hear about some authors getting away for a weekend or even a week just to write. That sounds more idyllic than I'm sure it is, but it doesn't currently fit with my life and responsibilities.

This last year, my writing schedule has had a lot of bumps, as my youngest son decided he wants to get up before 5:30 a.m. This disruption, under the providence of God and his perfect will, has helped me remember that my part-time "job" has neither an actual boss nor deadlines. At this stage, except for an occasional book review, my deadlines are usually self-inflicted. Therefore, I try not to resent it when my writing schedule shifts and "my time" is shortened or swallowed altogether. The keyword is *try*. I could do better at being okay with lost time, because this is precisely where the rubber of the perfect will of God meets the road. Later in the book, John talks in more detail about his writing schedule, which happens several weekdays during the mid-morning. This works well for John because he is at his sharpest during these hours. But because he does his writing in the church office during the work week, he still experiences interruptions common to bustling offices. It's not a competition, but I'd point out he has little to complain about since his interruptions are not so small and whiny and needing of a diaper change as my distractions.

How long do you plan to blog?

Related to how much time you'll spend blogging each week and month, it's wise to begin with some indication of how long you hope to blog. Is this something you'll get into for the next year, five years, or longer? I mention this because if you can't see yourself blogging for at least a year, I'm not sure how worthwhile it would be to set up a blog. I'm not suggesting the other extreme either, that you only begin to blog if you can make a twelve-year "for better, for worse" commitment. Who can know what the next dozen years will bring? Still, don't get into blogging if you only have three great ideas. Write them up as guest posts and submit them to other sites. If you enjoy the writing process, the posts find a readership, and you catch the blogging bug, then dive in.

How does blogging relate to your day job and family?

If I could go back and start my blog over again, I'm not sure what I would change about the blog itself. When I began blogging, the specifics of my role at church made my relationship with blogging murky. Besides, back then, I didn't know where my blogging would go. I didn't think through many of the questions we're discussing here, let alone have answers for them. It would have been odd, even arrogant, to have approached the leaders of our church asking them to give me the intellectual property rights for everything I produced. "Guys, I'm starting a blog, and I'm fairly sure I'm going to want all the royalties that come from it even when I repurpose sermons and other material originally written for our church. Sound okay?" That's some moxie right there. It would also have been pretty stupid. My blogging "career" continues to lose money, not make it. But some relationship between my day job and my hobby job existed whether I fully understood it or not. Because my paid work is pastoring and my blog centers on the Christian message of hope lived and applied and enjoyed, the potential is high for my blog to overlap with my work and my work to overlap with my blog. This can create confusion or at least ambiguity about when I'm working on each.

> For me, consistency is the hardest part of blogging. Ideas aren't as much of a problem as time is. Family and work responsibilities, finishing up a degree, reading enough to keep the idea tank filled, and taking time to rest adequately make it difficult at times to commit even just an hour or two to blog.
> – *Kris Sinclair,* _krissinclair.com_

For other bloggers the question is irrelevant because the potential for overlap does not exist. A math teacher in a public high school who blogs about how a Christian should approach politics has no overlap. Still, let me explore this math-teacher blogger a bit more. I'll call him Matt.

Matt teaches math from 8:00 a.m. to 4:00 p.m., and outside of that he blogs whenever he wants, so long as it's not during the time he's getting paid to instruct students. Matt might even be able to tinker with a post over his lunch break.

It is, after all, *his* lunch break. But the question of who the time belongs to cuts both ways. If the stated expectation is that third period is Matt's school planning period, during which school administrators expect him to create lessons and grade papers, then during that time it would be stealing from his employer and dishonoring to God to post about the latest abortion issues on his blog.

When I, however, work on a blog post over my lunch break, it is ambiguous whether I'm still working or not. Is blogging actually a break from working? It might be a break from one form of work to labor in another, but is it a break from the work my employer is paying me to do? That depends.

Let's go back to the example of a high school teacher. What if, instead, that teacher is a professor at a Christian university who teaches history and her blog is about approaching history from a Christian worldview. I'll call her Sarah. Often some of Sarah's lectures show up in blog posts. And just as frequently some lecture ideas first germinate as she waters her blog. Now, is it clear whether a blog post created on Sarah's lunch break is still a break from work? And what if that series of blog posts eventually becomes a book? I know enough to know that you don't just combine a few posts, and, voilà, out comes a book. It takes forever. But still, who owns those initial ideas and who owns the laptop?

I haven't said anything about having your spouse's encouragement and blessing to blog, but many of these same questions of time and effort apply, just in different ways. If you're a stay-at-home mom, the issues of intellectual property and what counts as work are not as contractually thorny, but they could become challenging from a relationship standpoint. This is why the more envisioning you can do before you launch a blog of how your blog will relate to your day job and your family, the better.

What is the topic, length, and frequency of your posts?

In the last chapter, John discussed the value of coming back to consistent themes in your posts. It helps readers know what to expect. Related to having a consistent theme, we'd encourage you to set a frequency for your posts. The most obvious rhythms are daily, a few times a week, weekly, bi-weekly, and monthly. If you're posting less than monthly, that's fine, but don't expect to build much of a relationship with regular readers because you can't have regular readers when you're not writing regularly.

Rather than starting with the frequency you want to achieve, it seems wiser to consider the amount of time you can reasonably allot to blogging and let that determine your posting schedule. If it takes you two hours to write each post, the goal of posting three times a week won't work if you only have three hours a week to blog.

I already mentioned that I only post once a week. For me, that's Tuesdays at 2:00 p.m. John posts two or three times each week, with a new article each Tuesday at 9:00 a.m., a weekly list of curated articles from around the web each Thursday at 9:00 a.m., and an occasional book review on Saturdays. Even his list of curated articles reflects the idea of staying on theme or brand. He typically shares a few articles broadly interesting to a Christian audience, articles about marriage and children, and common struggles like gossip or loneliness. The final article in his list is often a video, either a humorous one or some science factoid. I know we're coauthoring this book together, but he's never told me his schedule; I just know it from getting his emails each week for a few years and enjoying the rhythm.

Related to frequency is the length of your posts. I won't venture to say there is a "correct" word count that exists for blogs. It seems more people read shorter posts than longer, but at the same time, I keep reading that the current Google search algorithm favors longer posts.[2] My suggestion is to worry less about what others say is the right length and consider what length best fits your ability to write a post artfully. If this means your typical post is 600 words, great. If this means your typical post is 2,500, that's great too. But don't expect people to read your 2,500-word posts four times a week, even if you can crank them out. Ain't nobody got time for that. Also, expect to struggle to develop regular readers if each post varies widely in length and theme. Consistency in both will help your readers know what to expect from your blog and will go a long way in helping you develop a recognizable voice.

How will you promote your posts?

Finally, let's talk about promoting and sharing your posts. Promotion can be intimidating, even for experienced writers. Glenna Marshall writes, "I graduated with a degree in creative writing but spent the next twelve years blogging in secret because I was afraid to go public with my writing."[3] When I began my blog, I waited six months before telling anyone but a handful of readers, which felt like a long time. I struggle to even imagine the faithfulness required to blog in

---

[2] One expert suggests 1,750 words is the Google sweet spot (Amy Lupold Bair, *Blogging for Dummies, 7th ed.* [Hoboken, New Jersey: John Wiley & Sons, 2019], 190).

[3] Glenna Marshall, "Writing as Ministry," *GlennaMarshall.com*, February 28, 2019, https://www.glennamarshall.com/2019/02/28/writing-as-ministry/.

near secret for a dozen years. But whether we wait ten posts as Challies has suggested[4] or we wait a thousand posts—to be a blogger and not just an electronic journaler—we must do some amount of promotion, even if that means, like Marshall, simply pressing the button that turns our blog public.

The two main ways to promote your posts are social media and emailing your subscribers. Writing guest posts for other websites is another route, albeit less direct, to promoting your work. On your website you should be gathering emails from people who sign up for your blog, which we'll talk more about later in the book. If you're not doing this, you should. If you're using WordPress, you can email straight from that blogging platform. But if you're using something like Squarespace, you'll need to set up an account with an email subscription service, such as Mailchimp.

> Starting a blog is not a bad idea for anyone curious to try it. *Why not?* See what it's like and how God uses it to grow you and those who read your words. It can be such an effective tool in God's hands to help us worship and learn and grow and serve. – *Jen Oshman,* <u>jenoshman.com</u>

Some bloggers choose to email readers every time they publish (e.g., Carey Nieuwhof), and others don't, instead collecting several posts across a month or two and then emailing a round-up of the latest news from the blog (e.g., Jen Oshman and Glenna Marshall). There are strengths and weaknesses of each approach. With the "email-every-post" approach, readers don't miss a post. The downside is they quit opening your emails because of inbox fatigue. Emailing only every month or so avoids the fatigue but loses

---

[4] Tim Challies, "How To Get Started With Blogging in 2020," *Challies.com*, February 20, 2020, https://www.challies.com/articles/how-to-get-started-with-blogging-in-2020/.

immediacy. We can't tell you which is best for you, but you should think it through.

In terms of sharing your posts on social media, some of the same dynamics of "exposure" versus "fatigue" are at work. If you spent seven hours writing a post, please tell others about it. Blogging for God's glory shouldn't be misunderstood as blogging so that no one except God ever sees or knows your writing exists. That's the difference between journaling and blogging. Most bloggers reading this book are probably too shy at promoting their work because they've seen promotion done poorly by others. Find a balance and course-correct as needed.

Related to promoting posts, I should mention a word about updating posts when you notice a mistake or others point out the mistake for you. If your error involves more than a typo or minor clarification, you should add a note to either the top or bottom of the post flagging readers that, on a certain date, you updated the post to reflect a change. This is especially necessary when the mistake was not simply one of oversight or misprint but of judgment, falsehood, or tone. In this case, honoring God in your blogging may require you to apologize, perhaps even creating another post in addition to updating the old post.

Consider what Amy Lupold Bair writes in her book *Blogging for Dummies*: "Mistakes, big and little, are inevitable and upset people, but you can do a great deal to help yourself and your credibility by how you handle the mistake after you or your readers discover it."[5] If Bair can write this in a secular book, one that largely overlooks faith-based blogging, how much more shall I appeal to Christian bloggers—

---

[5] Amy Lupold Bair, *Blogging for Dummies*, 41.

those who know God's forgiveness in Christ—to admit when they have sinned and slandered? Knowing the good news of God's forgiveness is not simply important for one's entrance into God's family but for the empowerment to walk in the ways God's children ought to walk.

He Gives Sleep to His Beloved

In concrete language, Psalm 127 opens describing a world of vanity, not the vanity of decadence and arrogance but the vanity of futility. The psalm describes people who guard cities and build houses in vain; it describes those who rise early and stay up late in vain "eating the bread of anxious toil" (v. 2a). And yet, for all the sawdust floating into the air from their frenetic activity, when the dust falls to the ground, nothing has been accomplished.[6] "Unless the Lord builds the house," Solomon writes, "those who build it labor in vain" (v. 1). The movers and shakers move and shake, but the needle doesn't move. They blog early and late, seeking to build traffic, optimizing posts for search engines, but unless the Lord is behind the blog, they post in vain.

> When family life gets busy, or church commitments need more time, I can rest in the truth that the blogging world will go on without me. Bloggers aren't needed, but we do *get to* worship. – Brianna Lambert, *lookingtotheharvest.com*

In verse 2 Solomon continues by writing that God "gives sleep to his beloved." In a world of frantic side-hustles and sometimes greasy self-promotion, God has a better way. He gives sleep to his beloved. If you don't feel like you can get adequate sleep most nights because you have so much to do,

---

[6] I might have heard Paul Washer say something like this in a sermon once—using the sawdust metaphor—but I can't remember for sure.

so many blog posts to write, so many readers to reach, so many ideas you just have to get out there into the world, it might be because you're not blogging for God's glory but your own.

The imagery at the start of the psalm is about those protecting a city, which they do in vain because, we presume, they do it in their own strength and not the Lord's. But at the end of the psalm, the ones who sleep and raise a family, activities that seem so ordinary, in the end have grown children launched out like arrows from a quiver and fathers standing unashamed before his enemies at the gates of the city (vv. 3–5). In short, the tasks people tried to achieve by the sweat of their brows, they accomplish by following the perfect will of God, all while catching more sleep and eating less hurried meals than their peers.

And so will you when you let the Lord build your blog.

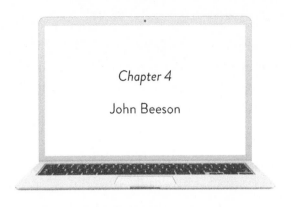

Chapter 4

John Beeson

OBSTACLES

What Hurdles Will I Encounter?

B logging isn't easy. Right now you can go on Amazon and pick up a half-dozen books that tell you just how easy it is and how much money you're going to make from it. But the reality is the vast majority of blogs fizzle out and die within a year of their launch, and even those that continue are rarely profitable financially. It's unlikely that your blog will become such a rocketship that Zondervan, Moody, Thomas Nelson, or LifeWay knock down your door with a publishing deal.

I don't say that as a discouragement. It certainly has happened. I think of Justin Taylor and Ann Voskamp as counterexamples.

What do you do when you've written a string of posts that has received little response? How are you going to push through when you pitch an article to a larger outlet to try to expand your platform but are rejected? What do you do when you *are* published by larger platforms but don't get the response or boost in readership you hoped for? How do you stay encouraged when the unsubscribe list is longer than the subscribe list?

Every one of these discouragements has been felt by both of us.

We've had many posts rejected by platforms we thought they would be perfectly suited for. We've also had posts published on larger platforms only to realize they hardly drove any traffic to our sites.

How are you going to persevere? What is going to help you overcome the many obstacles?

Make Your Bed

In James Clear's helpful book *Atomic Habits*, Clear explains how we can develop what he calls "atomic habits," that is, habits that become ingrained in who you are so that tremendous energy isn't spent executing the tasks.

Clear gives some strange but helpful advice about starting and following through on new habits. He says the key is not just doing the thing but becoming the type of person who does the thing. To do so, Clear encourages incremental steps in becoming that type of person. For instance, Clear encourages that before you jump into hour-long workouts, just show up to the gym, walk in, and then leave. In other words, you start to become the type of person who goes to the gym every day. And then you actually become that person.[1]

There are all sorts of habits like this that are already present in your life. I'm a bed-maker now, but I wasn't always a

---

[1] James Clear, *Atomic Habits: An Easy & Proven Way to Build Good Habits & Break Bad Ones* (New York: Penguin, 2018), 159–68.

bed-maker. In high school my parents frequently nagged me about making my bed. It didn't matter to me at the time, and I didn't understand why it mattered to them. Making my bed was literally and figuratively a chore.

And then I went to college. It clicked. When all I had was that shared one-bedroom abode, making my bed mattered to me. Walking into rooms of both bed-makers and non-bed-makers, I realized I wanted to be a bed-maker. To me, they seemed more focused, more put together, and more motivated. Making my bed made me feel like I was starting my day right, like things were in their place, and my concentration could be spent on going after the next task. And so, most every day, my bed was, and is, made.

Working out has been an off-and-on habit for me. But in the seasons where I'm faithful, it's not only built into my task list and schedule, it is treated with almost the same degree of importance as other significant tasks, and it is as immovable from my schedule as a staff meeting would be. Failure to prioritize your blogging schedule can lead to sporadic, almost manic blogging highs and lows. Chris Thomas notes this was one of his chief struggles in the early iterations of his blogs. "When the stars aligned," he writes, "I would produce a flurry of content and push it all out as soon as was possible. Then, more often than not, would follow silence that rivaled the intertestamental period."[2]

A blogging schedule is the secret sauce of long-term and faithful blogging. Where does it fit in your calendar? For Benjamin, his writing time is early in the morning. For me, Tuesday, Wednesday, and Friday mid-mornings are my

---

[2] Chris Thomas, "Why I Started Blogging. Why I Stopped. And Why I Started Again." *The Ploughman's Rest*, January 10, 2019, http://ploughmansrest.com/blog/2019/1/10/why-i-started-blogging-why-i-stopped-and-why-a-started-again.

writing times. I divide this between sermon preparation and blog writing. I find the two are helpful companions. In general, I would say that I devote around three to four hours a week to writing for my blog. It's hard to pin that down, though, as there are weeks I will write a couple of posts and other weeks I don't write any posts, but ideas are germinating in other ways. Every week I'm doing some sort of writing.

Just as important as writing posts is the germination of ideas for them. Your best thoughts are those that you've sat with for a while. My best posts are rarely thought of on the spot and then banged out over a couple of hours. Instead, I find that my best writing happens when I tease out an idea that has been percolating for a couple of weeks or months.

My germination file is in Evernote. That file contains a growing list of ideas for blog posts. Some of those ideas are a phrase, while others are a paragraph. They come to me in all sorts of ways, and once I have the idea, they develop as I read, think, and pray. My log of post ideas sits at roughly fifty today. But not all are ready to be written. And some will never be written.

Using Clear's process, I would encourage you to open a document and write down one idea for a post every day for a week. Start becoming a blogger in how you think about the world. On weeks two through four, continue adding new ideas to your idea document, and then spend a half hour, two or three times a week, beginning to form a few of those ideas into posts.

Once you have your feet under you with these habits, set a time frame for what your commitment to blogging will be. What date are you hoping to reach as a deadline? Again, a gym analogy is helpful. When I use the cardio machines in the gym, I have to set the timer. If I don't plug in thirty minutes into the Stairmaster, I know I'll convince myself after fifteen minutes I've done plenty.

Be Faithful to Your Audience

We've spent some time already talking about your audience. Your audience will at one point or another become a challenge for you. One series of posts I wrote began to get a decent amount of traction with some of my unbelieving friends. It was a lot of fun. And it was tempting. "Wait a second," I thought, "maybe *this* is the group I should be writing for. Maybe I can write a blog engaging questions unbelievers ask." But while I love engaging unbelievers and entering into this sort of dialogue, I'm currently called to write primarily for my local church.

You are likely to get traction with different groups from time to time, and you'll need to think through whether the traction ought to represent a change of direction for you or whether you should appreciate the engagement you received around those posts while continuing to cultivate the relationship with your primary audience. There will be times when a new direction and audience is called for, and there will be times where a new direction and audience would be foolish.

There is a local church where the senior pastor underwent a significant theological transformation. The church was Pentecostal in its roots and Arminian in its theology, but the pastor began to read the work of reformed pastors like R. C. Sproul and John Piper, and that changed him. Instead of walking through a process of discernment with his elders, staff, and leaders, the pastor brought the congregation into his theological transformation midstream. He began preaching on the doctrines of grace and urging his congregation to follow. It caused massive upheaval. He thought he could transform his message and maintain his same audience. That rarely works.

If you are working through a theological or philosophical transformation, particularly if it is combustible, do so slowly and with care. Seek counsel about whether you should share your thoughts or whether you need some time. You might not be ready. Or you might need to lead your audience with care. Some posts I've written have been shelved because, with counsel, I determined they wouldn't serve my audience. On the other hand, I've written on some fairly controversial topics (I wrote a series on non-violence and a series on worship preferences, for example) but have done so only after counsel.

> It took me a long time to realize that there's no intrinsic relationship between how passionately a writer feels and how much time they spend on a particular piece to its impact on readers. – *Samuel James*, *letterandliturgy.com*

The opposite is also true. You might think you're writing to one audience only to have a different audience respond. That is fine. Be self-aware and have enough emotional intelligence to be able to read who your audience is and see and respond to them appropriately.

When I moved from Princeton, New Jersey, back to Tucson, Arizona, I misjudged the massive shift in audience. Princeton was a highly educated and cultured audience because it's the home of Princeton University. Having grown up in Tucson, I assumed I understood the locals and they would understand me. I was wrong. It took me a couple of years to be able to adjust my preaching and writing style to fit the audience I was writing to. Princeton cares about tradition, history, and logic. Tucson cares about autonomy, personal connection, and authenticity. These differences are matters of degree, of course. It's not as though Tucsonans want sloppy argumentation and Princetonians want inauthenticity, but there is certainly a hierarchy of values. The same is true of your blogging audience. Over time you will be able to discern what your audience values most and how you can best deliver that to them.

There can also be some risks to letting your audience have too much influence on your writing. One of the most-read series of posts I've ever written was about the near collapse of our marriage and its miraculous healing. While I don't have a suitcase full of devastating personal stories, I was certainly reminded of the value of connecting with my audience as a fellow traveler and struggler.

As a pastor, I need to show discretion where struggles involve the confidentiality of my congregants. However, where appropriate, and with consent, sharing personal stories helps connect at the heart level with readers.

Impostor Syndrome

If you're fortunate, you'll have moments where a post goes viral. My kids and co-workers still tease me that I'm John Piper's best friend because a guest post of mine at The Gospel Coalition ended up being read widely (by my standards) and John Piper was kind enough to commend it with a generous tweet. Unsurprisingly, the human heart struggles with success even more than it struggles with failure. When you have your five minutes of fame, be prepared for a collision of emotions:

- **Excitement.** You're going to get a hit of joy, and that's a good thing. Allow yourself to smile and be gracious to those who give you a pat on the back.
- **Impostor syndrome.** Psychologists call it "impostor phenomenon." It's the sneaking feeling that you are a fraud and that your success can't be duplicated.
- **Pride.** Interestingly, even while feeling you are a fraud, daydreams might pop up that you'll make it big. Maybe this is the new normal. Maybe you will be the next Ann Voskamp or Kevin DeYoung. That book you've been dreaming of writing is going to be read by tens of thousands, not merely tens.
- **Discouragement.** You begin to realize that your shooting-star moment hasn't fundamentally changed your platform. After the flood of eyes to your post, your audience shrinks back to about the same size, with one-time readers fading away. Normal engagement for a post now feels disappointing. You might even feel used; why won't readers who found your writing helpful sign up? Why won't they return?

Our hearts are so fickle. Success and failure alike can bring out the worst in us. But these moments are opportunities for self-understanding and sanctification if you allow God to use them. The glory that is brought to God is not proportionate to your subscription list.

The Challenge of Social Media

Perhaps one of the most surprising challenges for a blogger is how difficult it is to get social media to work for you. Without question, you should use social media. It's too ubiquitous to ignore. I use Facebook the most, with Twitter, Instagram, and Pinterest getting lesser degrees of usage. They're useful but limited instruments. Frankly, none of those platforms has had a significant impact on the growth of my blog.

It feels defeating when you have the tools to get your message out to a broad group but ever-constricting algorithms keep suppressing you. "Keep on keeping on" and realize that the best focus you can have is on creating the best content you can.

There is always going to be the "next thing" out there. All sorts of platforms have had their minute, from Periscope to QZone to Myspace, from Snapchat to Reddit, and who knows what will be next? Recognize from the beginning that you won't ever be able to keep up. Pick what you do best naturally, figure out where your audience already is, and spend your time there.

> One of the fastest ways to get discouraged is to pour your heart and soul into a piece of writing and see it go nowhere online. It's so frustrating to see clickbait get passed around like crazy, only to see your own hard-fought posts go to the internet to die. – *Melissa Edgington, yourmomhasablog.com*

Early in my ministry in Princeton I decided to create brief YouTube videos reflecting on a biblical thought and applying it to life. They were poorly done and didn't get much traction, but I'm glad I tried them out. Since then, YouTube has grown immensely and is now a mammoth platform with massive opportunities.

I could imagine that it might make sense for me to expend time and energy on YouTube in the future, but for now I feel as though the best contribution I can make with my skill set is through my blog. It seems to me that even if I branch out, the anchor of my creative work will be my preaching and blogging ministry.

What do you want your base to be? Maybe you have skills to host a podcast or start a YouTube channel. Those are great and important endeavors! Be thoughtful about what the cornerstone to your creative work will be. It's not that your creative pursuits can't change, but every change you walk through with your audience will require patience on their behalf and new energies on yours. Pick what you naturally do best, and start cranking away.

Breaking Your Writer's Block

One of the biggest challenges for many writers is the dreaded writer's block. How are you going to overcome this challenge? Here are what I've found to be some of the best tips for overcoming writer's block:

1. **Choose habit over passion.** The more writing becomes an overflow of habit as opposed to the overflow of passion, the more you will begin to beat back writer's block. Most early writers write out of passion, but that passion will dry up. When it does, how will you continue writing? In fact, like visual art and music, the majority of people connect writing to an overflow of passion. But passion is a fickle friend. And furthermore, when you only write out of passion, your writing voice is likely to be overwrought and not as trustworthy. Write, write, write. Start journaling, start writing responses to blog posts you've read, start writing book reviews—just write!

2. **Write poorly.** Don't be afraid to write poorly. Even if you just have a quarter of an idea, it's better to write poorly about a poorly formed idea than to not write

at all. You'll likely find that as you write the idea begins to develop in ways you didn't expect. As Michael Hyatt says, "Perfectionism is the mother of procrastination."[3]

3. **Be a learner.** Writing is a conduit for idea formation, and ideas flow in the pipes of others' ideas. Listen to podcasts, read blogs and books, take an online class, and have engaging conversations. Each of these forms of learning will generate ideas for your writing.

4. **Stay ahead.** There will be weeks when you get slammed or your well runs dry. Start ahead with your blog and stay ahead. Have posts in the bank when you launch your blog. My ideal is to write my post, sit on it for a couple weeks, come back to it, edit it myself, and then send it to my editors a couple of weeks before I post it on my blog. That time is critical in helping me shape and clarify the argument and ensure that what I'm writing isn't reactionary or caught up in the news cycle or cultural storm.

5. **Don't be afraid to reappropriate.** If you're a fellow pastor, I encourage you to avoid using your blog as a second version of your sermon. Instead, use your blog to research and reinforce a subject you couldn't cover as deeply as you would've hoped in a sermon. Similarly, if you are presenting something for a class or for work, don't be afraid to revisit the same subject in a way that would benefit your audience.

---

[3] Michael Hyatt, *Platform: Get Noticed in a Noisy World* (Nashville: Thomas Nelson, 2012), 94.

When I Run, I Feel God's Wrath

I've had a handful of people ask me about what it takes to start a blog. I always respond by asking what they are passionate about and what they want to communicate. I often offer them an opportunity to write for my blog. I tell them I would be happy to edit, provide feedback, and if it would serve the audience well, post their article. A few have taken me up on the offer, but many haven't followed through. I understand. It's one thing to think about the idea of writing; it's another to put in the work to write that idea on paper. The reality is that writing is a discipline and a hard discipline at that.

If you start blogging with the primary purpose to grow your platform or to experience the high of being seen and heard by a crowd, you will be sorely disappointed. I can't tell you how many times I've posted something I was really excited about only to hear crickets. No, that's not true. Crickets at least emit a noise. The life-changing words I had poured my heart into were met with silence.

One individual who asked me about blogging spoke of the desire to get their story "out there" to have a platform to share experiences and "make a difference." As I dug, I heard someone who longed to make a name and an impact but whose passion (and likely skill) for the medium of writing didn't match their desire to create change.

The only way you will be able to persevere is by having your *why* big enough and clear enough before you. The only way you will be able to persevere is by having the face of your *who* before you and caring for them as you write. Chasing traffic and a platform will cannibalize your energy. Don't expect the day-in and day-out of the journey to be sufficient.

Two years ago my dad pulled together a group of friends to run a Tough Mudder with him. If you're not familiar, a Tough Mudder is a ten-mile race with roughly twenty-four obstacles interspersed throughout. I'm not a runner at all, but I love my dad, and it sounded like it could be a good bonding experience. I decided that I ought to train so the group wouldn't be slowed down too much. And so, I began to run a bit.

The famed Eric Liddell of *Chariots of Fire* once said, "When I run, I feel [God's] pleasure." I've never, ever experienced that. I don't have a runner's mindset, and at 6'3" and 215 pounds, I certainly don't have a runner's physique. When I run, I feel God's wrath.[4]

Okay, that might be a bit of an overstatement, but you get the point. Anyway, I began to churn out runs in preparation for the Tough Mudder. I ran alone in my neighborhood with podcasts and audiobooks in my ears. A mile at first, then two, then three, and finally, very painfully, I worked my way up to ten miles in preparation for the race. It was a very ugly ten miles, but there it was.

And then the day of the race came. We drove up to a carnival-like atmosphere. People were dressed up in costumes, and loud music blared through massive speakers. Energy drinks were shoved into your hand at the starting line, and photographers bounced around the course, snapping pictures of muddied, smiling participants. It was as if basic training and a college football tailgate had a child. It was a ton of fun. And while I didn't turn into Eric Liddell, running those ten miles with my dad and buddies, surrounded by

---

[4] Benjamin pointed out that in Drew Dyck's book *Your Future Self Will Thank You* (p. 190) he says something similar: "God made me slow. And when I run, I feel His displeasure." I haven't read Dyck's book, but I'm sure it's excellent!

throngs of smiling people and thumping music, was a heck of a lot more fun than beating the pavement alone in my neighborhood.

Friends, blogging is a lot more like beating the pavement alone in your neighborhood than it is running the Tough Mudder. I love Michael Hyatt's advice, "You will never see the full path. The important thing to do is the next right thing."[5]

Paul, the Marathon Runner

Paul must have had similar feelings about running because he uses it as a metaphor for the doggedness of his ministry. In 1 Corinthians 9, he says,

> For though I am free from all, I have made myself a servant to all, that I might win more of them. To the Jews I became as a Jew, in order to win Jews. To those under the law I became as one under the law (though not being myself under the law) that I might win those under the law. To those outside the law I became as one outside the law (not being outside the law of God but under the law of Christ) that I might win those outside the law. To the weak I became weak, that I might win the weak. I have become all things to all people, that by all means I might save some. I do it all for the sake of the gospel, that I may share with them in its blessings.
>
> Do you not know that in a race all the runners run, but only one receives the prize? So run that you may obtain it. Every athlete exercises self-control in all things. They do it to receive a perishable wreath, but we an

---

[5] Michael Hyatt, *Platform*, 38, emphasis removed.

imperishable. So I do not run aimlessly; I do not box as one beating the air. But I discipline my body and keep it under control, lest after preaching to others I myself should be disqualified.

Even if you're familiar with this passage, my hunch is that you thought of it as two different passages. In verses 19–23 Paul's passion to make an impact on his audience is so deep that he imaginatively makes whatever connection he can with them. Paul ministered to dozens more audiences than I have ministered to, and they were all just as diverse as Princeton and Tucson. And yet Paul knew that if he worked hard enough, he could make meaningful connections with each audience.

The next section appears to take quite a turn. In verses 24–27 Paul shares his commitment to sacrifice whatever is necessary to beat his body into submission that he might receive the prize after running the race.

When you read this passage fully, it's clear that, for Paul, part of the difficult discipline of running the race well is stewarding his gifts in the service of his audience. Paul's grueling marathon *is* giving himself to his readers.

If God has called you to the ministry of blogging, run steady, run hard, and strengthen your discipline that God might use you to win some to himself.

Blogging is fraught with challenges. But I believe your *why* is bigger than those challenges. You can and will glorify God as you persevere and live out his good purposes for your good calling.

Chapter 5

Benjamin Vrbicek

WIDGETS

What Behind-the-Scenes Details Do I Need to Know?

They say "you get what you pay for."

My wife and I found this out the hard way. By current standards, we did the unthinkable. Our wedding was filmed by a friend who didn't have a business or background in videography. He was a decent amateur photographer, so we assumed he could also work a video camera. We were wrong. His payment for filming our wedding was a t-shirt from our university's track and field team. (My wife and I met as college teammates.) Now, our payment to him was a "nice t-shirt," if I can say that. It was one of those Nike dri-fit shirts we used as part of our official warm-up uniform. But we certainly got what we paid for. While a professional string quartet played Pachelbel's "Canon in D" and my soon-to-be father-in-law walked his only daughter down the aisle, Spielberg decided *this* was the perfect moment to reposition the camera, so he picked up the tripod and moved to a new spot. The whole time Brooke walked down the aisle, the camera filmed the ceiling with shaky hands. He repositioned just in time to catch the giving away of the bride. This is pretty much how the rest of the footage goes.

Skimping on blogging costs will have fewer noticeable consequences and can usually be fixed retroactively with upgrades—unlike our wedding video. Still, when you opt for a free blogging website, you're limiting what your website can do. And whether you realize it or not, using several of the free websites will brand you as an amateur before anyone has read a single word.

Blogging Costs

I spend about $350 each year on blogging. This does not include editing costs for when I need an article to be more polished than I can achieve on my own. The money includes the cost of the website platform, email service, and domain names. I currently use Squarespace to blog, Mailchimp to send emails, and manage two purchased domains. Let's spend some time thinking about each of these expenses.

Domain Name

Just as a home and business have a physical address, so does a website. The domain name is the address where people find you on the internet. Often people call it the URL, which stands for Uniform Resource Locator, but I had to look that up to be certain because no one ever says the acronym in long-form. Look at it like this: the website domain name is the city and street address where your website lives, and the URL is like the specific house on a specific street in a specific city and state. For example, I live on Hillcrest Road in Harrisburg, Pennsylvania. That's like the domain name. But there are a bunch of houses on Hillcrest Road. That's where the full URL comes in handy. The specific house number is the full URL.

To explain this better, I'll use the following domain name as an example:

bloggingforGodsglory.com

We can liken the *.com* at the end of the domain name to a specific "state." There is a Hillcrest Road in Harrisburg, Pennsylvania, and a Hillcrest Road in Springfield, Illinois, just as you have

bloggingforGodsglory.*com* and

bloggingforGodsglory.*org*

and a host of other endings, or "states" if you will (*.me, .co, .blog*, etc.). The full URL points to specific places on the street. So, for example,

bloggingforGodsglory.com/about

bloggingforGodsglory.com/home

point you to the "About Page" and "Home Page." When you purchase a domain name, you purchase a street on which you can choose to build as many houses as you'd like. To put it all together, the relationships look like this:

Country	Site name	Fan and Flame
State	Domain	benjaminvrbicek.com
Address	URL	www.benjaminvrbicek.com/home

I own two domain names, *fanandflame.com* and *benja-minvrbicek.com*. I used the first one for several years because it is the name I gave my blog, which is an allusion to 2 Timothy 1:6, where Paul tells Timothy to "fan into flame the gift of God." I take this command to "fan into flame" to mean that the young pastor Timothy must do whatever was necessary to keep the fire burning. If only embers remain, well then, you get on your hands and knees, put your nose in the kindling, and blow. Never mind the smoke searing your eyes, you keep the fire alive; you don't let the fire become extinguished; you toil to make it grow. I chose the blog name "Fan and Flame" because I wanted to fan into flame joy and hope in the gospel through my writing.

When you go to fanandflame.com today, however, you'll immediately be redirected to benjaminvrbicek.com. For several years I resisted the idea of having a website with my name in the URL because it felt pretentious. I'm mostly over that now, but at the time I changed the address of my blog, I had enough guest post articles linking to fanandflame.com that I felt the need to keep both domains.

Let me return to my earlier comment about being branded as an amateur before anyone has read a single word on your blog. That comment had to do with your URL. I'll use the free websites from WordPress.com as an example. If you get a free WordPress website, WordPress puts its name in the URL. For example,

fanandflame.*wordpress*.com or

benjaminvrbicek.*wordpress*.com.

As a blogger, you receive a free website out of this deal, and WordPress receives free advertising. But, again, it makes you look like a rookie. Paying the $30–40 each year will give you a clean, ad-free URL. If you want to begin blogging with a free website as you test the waters, that's fine. But once you dip more than a toe in the water, just buy the domain name for a year and ditch the free advertising for WordPress.[1]

Before moving on, there are a few things to mention. Domain names are typically purchased yearly, so stay on top of this. Don't let payment for your domain name lapse because someone else might take it. Most website companies will help you with this by setting up automatic annual payment and sending emails to let you know when it's time to re-up. Keeping the domain sold to you is in their interest too. While you can buy a domain name directly through various websites, most blogging platforms allow you to purchase the domain name through their platform when you set up your blog.

Blogging Platforms

Once you have the domain name, you will need to choose a blogging platform. A blogging platform is sometimes called a content management system or CMS. There are many to pick from: WordPress.com, WordPress.org, Squarespace, Blogger, Medium, Wix, and many others. Since so many exist and new options continuously pop up, I won't evaluate each platform's strengths and weaknesses. I will, however, mention what to consider when choosing a blogging platform.

First, know your level of technical ability and choose accordingly. If you are intimidated by technical work, stay

---

[1] When talking about URLs, often the prefix includes either http or https. The "s" stands for secure, which means you'll want to make sure you set up your blog with this prefix by following the necessary steps. Having a secure URL improves safety, SEO traffic, and design.

away from WordPress.org, which I'll explain more about below. A quick Google search of "best blogging platforms" will help you get a sense of the right platform for you. For example, if you plan to sell products from your blog, some platforms handle e-commerce better than others.

Second, choose a website platform that has sharp, appealing templates. To use an analogy, a blogging platform is like choosing a department store to buy an outfit from, like J. C. Penney or Macy's. A template is like choosing an outfit from within a store.

> Do everything you feasibly can to ensure that your website looks good and is fast and responsive. It's sobering to think about how much good thinking and writing is hindered by poor design and bad technical infrastructure.
>
> – Kris Sinclair, _krissinclair.com_

Not to be obnoxious, but we can press the analogy further. The third step, once you've picked a platform and a template, is to customize your template. This is like picking out pants (your website footer), a shirt (your website header), and many other details such as menu bars and email subscription forms, which are like belts and shoes. The "department store" (blogging platform) determines the number of "outfits" (templates) you can choose from and the degree to which those outfits are customizable. Brooks Brothers sells suits, not sweatpants, and Macy's sells both.

Once you have your blog dressed the way you like, you will probably be eager to go public. But you should check a few things before you walk out the door. It's important to confirm that your website still looks good in two different scenarios. You'll want to confirm your website displays correctly on various internet browsers—at least the three major browsers of Chrome, Safari, and Internet Explorer.

It is also important to confirm that your blog looks good when viewed from a desktop (or laptop) computer, a tablet, and a mobile device. In fact, websites not designed to handle mobile traffic are penalized in Google's search algorithm.[2] Designing your website for different sources of website traffic is a big topic, so I'll explain a bit more.

The two ways to design a website for mobile traffic are to build either a "responsive" or "adaptive" website. A responsive website adjusts the layout of the website based on the screen resolution. An adaptive website is more like designing two websites, one shown to desktop users and another to those on mobile devices. Bloggers using templates will end up taking the "responsive" route, so you'll want to be aware of the term and look for it as you browse templates.

If using a desktop computer, you can experience what it feels like to have a website designed for traffic from various sources. Visit any professional, popular website from a desktop. Then click and hold one of the corners of the browser window and drag the window to make the browser's width smaller. As you make the browser window smaller, the website will seamlessly change layout based on size. As you make the browsing window roughly the size of a tablet, the website will shift to a "tablet layout." As you keep shrinking the window, the website will jump seamlessly to a "mobile layout." This is what you want your website to do because, while most people design their website on a desktop, the majority of traffic comes through mobile devices.

Around 55% of the traffic on my website comes from mobile devices, 35% from desktops, and 10% from tablets. The

---

[2] Ventura Web Design, https://www.venturawebdesign.com/responsive-vs-mobile-website-design/. You can test the mobile readiness of your website with Google's tester: https://search.google.com/test/mobile-friendly.

percentage of mobile traffic becomes especially high whenever I have a guest post on a more prominent website. I suspect this is the case because that website shares their posts via social media accounts, which most people see on phones and, in turn, readers eventually click over to my website from my bio at the bottom of the article. The click-over-from-bio happens less often than you might think, though.

The moral of the story is to ensure whatever template you use works well with mobile traffic. If over half of the people looking at your website have a lousy reading experience because they have to zoom in and out with their thumbs to make articles readable, it won't be long before they quit reading. Imagine going to a grocery store that keeps different kinds of fruit at the top of different ladders. For apples, you climb one ladder. For bananas, you climb another. It won't be long before people shop elsewhere no matter how good the fruit tastes.

Before moving on to emails, there is one more topic to consider: hosting. For many websites, hosting is a non-issue because the only way to use the blogging platform is when they host your blog for you. Hosting refers to where all the blogging data is stored. Think about hosting like storing pictures on your phone. If you only have your pictures stored (i.e., hosted) on your phone, a dropped or stolen phone could lose everything. But if you periodically sync your pictures to a "cloud" storage system, your pictures are stored securely on a supercomputer inside a building called a data center; you never have to worry about permanently losing your selfies. Cloud storage, however, is not the same as buying insurance for your phone, which helps you replace a broken phone but won't necessarily restore the data on your phone. Only storing your pictures outside of your phone keeps them safe. This same kind of backup cloud protection is what bloggers call hosting.

Be aware, though, that unless your blog is self-hosted,[3] the host technically owns the content. For my website, Squarespace hosts everything for me. There isn't even an option to self-host, an option that most often comes into play when people choose to use a specific form of WordPress.

Speaking of WordPress, there are two main WordPress products, WordPress.*com* and WordPress.*org*. They are similar but different in significant ways. It's been said that WordPress.com is like renting an apartment, and Word-Press.org is like owning a home. When you rent, you can customize only a limited number of things. You can pick the furniture you put in each room and the artwork you hang on the walls. In some rental agreements, you might even be able to paint the walls any color you like. But when you rent, you can't choose to knock down walls to give the kitchen and living room the "open concept" feel that's so popular right now. When you own a home, nearly everything is customizable. You can knock down any wall you wish. The downside of owning, however, is that you might accidentally knock down a load-bearing wall, a costly mistake. And if you own your home and the water heater breaks, you can't call the landlord to fix the problem because *you* are the landlord. Again, this is the difference between the two forms of WordPress.[4]

When you use WordPress.org to own the site, you're the one responsible for figuring out hosting and keeping plugins

---

[3] The term *self-hosted* can mislead. To self-host a blog does not necessarily mean you only store all of your blog's information on your computer; for most bloggers, self-hosting means hiring a company to keep all of your data secure for a small monthly subscription, typically around \$4–8.

[4] WPBeginner.com is a good website to help you make the most of WordPress.org.

functioning correctly. Again, hosting is where all the data is saved. There are several companies to choose from, such as Bluehost, HostGator, and SiteGround, as well as Flywheel and WP Engine, which are dedicated specifically to Word-Press.[5]

This leads to the topic of website plugins and widgets. Plugins are the little bits of software that enable your website to perform tasks, like helping your posts appear higher in web searches or tracking the metrics of your website in a visual display when you login as an admin to WordPress. Your website might only need a handful of plugins to customize your template, but there are thousands available, all performing different functions, such as improving your rank in search engines, reducing spam in your comments, increasing your website loading speed, and so on.

Widgets are similar to plugins in that they also improve the functionality of your website, but whereas plugins live in the background of the website, widgets are visible. For example, a widget might change the layout of your website footer or add a search function to your sidebar.

Plugins and widgets tend to be *open-source*, which means designers created them for use by the public without violating copyrights. While the ability to choose the best plugins and widgets for each application might be desirable, it also opens you up to choosing an inferior bit of code. For example, you might want a plugin or widget that allows your blog to play audio files, but let's say you choose a particular one that doesn't look good on a mobile device or with a specific internet browser. Frustrating, right?

---

[5] Hosting is one of several factors that influence the loading speed of your website.

The highest level of owning a website involves writing CSS and HTML code. If you want to, you can build a website from scratch. I'm going to leave that discussion alone because it would quickly go over my head, and those who would understand the material don't need me to write about it anyway.

For many authors, this technical side of blogging is the pits; you want a clean website but don't know how to create one. My only advice is not to bail on blogging just because you can't set up your blog effectively. Recruit a friend or hire a pro to help you. Then focus on what makes a blog a blog: the writing.

Email Services

As with blogging platforms, several email services exist to help bloggers communicate with readers: Mailchimp, ConvertKit, Constant Contact, MailerLite, Emma, and others. I'll be brief on this point, but allow me to stress the importance of having an email list. Author and book marketing guru Tim Grahl notes that if you were to ask successful marketers to "choose between their email list or all of their other marketing assets combined (Facebook, Google+, Twitter, their blog, their podcast), they'd pick the email list every time."[6] Michael Hyatt agrees: "People often ask, 'What's the most important thing I need to do in building my platform?' My answer? 'Develop a robust email list.'"[7] Not to belabor the point, but Donald Miller says that though he has hundreds of thousands of Twitter followers and nearly as many

---

[6] Tim Grahl, *Book Launch Blueprint: The Step-by-Step Guide to a Bestselling Launch* (Independently Published, 2015), 16–17.
[7] Michael Hyatt, "A Step by Step Guide for Creating a Magnetic Email Incentive," *MichaelHyatt.com*, June 9, 2014, https://michaelhyatt.com/email-incentive.

Facebook followers, "all my social media platforms combined don't perform anywhere close to sending out an update or offer via e-mail."[8] Grahl, Hyatt, Miller, and many others say this because having emails allows you to talk directly to people who want your content.

When you send emails from your email service, they will come from a specific address, so make it professional. The ideal is an email branded with symmetry to your website, for example, info@yourwebsite.com or yourname@your-website.com. If you don't have an email like this, just create one with Gmail containing your first and last name.

When you begin collecting emails, your email service provider will likely ask you whether you want *single opt-in* or *double opt-in*. Double requires a person to click within an email that is generated and sent as soon as he or she subscribes. When the person clicks the link, the double opt-in is complete. Single opt-in does not require this step. The advantage of single is ease and speed, while the downside involves potentially fake emails and mistyped emails getting on your list. Additionally, with single opt-in your emails can perpetually be marked as spam and never read because the subscriber didn't have to find that first email. Double requires people to

> Cultivating attention in an oversaturated world isn't easy. I'm not going viral with any of what I write. Although, with my email list and social media accounts I have been able to build relationships with readers and grow a following of people who know what to expect from my writing. This has been key for me not giving up. – *Kevin Halloran, kevinhalloran.net*

---

[8] Donald Miller, *Building a StoryBrand: Clarify Your Message So Customers Will Listen* (New York: HarperCollins, 2017), 183.

acknowledge the first email, which might also force them to first look in a spam or junk folder.

Whether you know the acronym or not, if you have signed up to an email list, you've seen CAPTCHA, those tests at the end of a form to confirm you are a human, not a robot. A CAPTCHA test might require you simply to check a box, or do something more complex, such as identify and retype a word written with a goofy font, solve a simple math problem, or count how many tiles include pictures of crosswalks.

As I already mentioned, I currently use Mailchimp for email and Squarespace for blogging. (John does too, by the way, so we're not very diversified in our knowledge base, although I blogged with both versions of WordPress for a few years each.) Using Squarespace and Mailchimp together is nice because the two companies "talk" well with each other. Squarespace has an agreement with Mailchimp that lets users send information back and forth between the two. For example, when a reader subscribes using the button on my Squarespace website, my email subscriber list in Mailchimp immediately updates. This triggers Mailchimp to send the automated welcome email I wrote.

Lead Magnets

Now that we have an email service picked, how do you find subscribers? In addition to writing excellent posts, providing an appealing *lead magnet* is a great way to get readers to subscribe. A lead magnet is the item you promise to give away in return for a reader giving you his or her email address. The lead magnet could be an ebook, infographic, interview audio recording, or whatever you think might nudge someone to subscribe. Typically the offer of "subscribe to get new posts" or "subscribe to get my monthly newsletter" is not enough, especially when every blog seems to have similar marketing.

When people subscribe to your blog, set up an automatic email that allows subscribers to get what you promised in the lead magnet. You do this through your email service. If you don't have an ebook, you might be able to take a few of your most popular posts and turn them into something worthwhile. The ebook doesn't have to be lengthy. To give you an example, let's say you wrote a series of five blog posts about how to strengthen your marriage while you have young children, or maybe you wrote a series of posts about how to preach the gospel from Old Testament books. You can easily rewrite that series so that the posts fit well together, make a book cover, save it as a PDF, offer to give it away as a lead magnet, and include it in your welcome email. If the creation of a short ebook feels too daunting, don't hesitate to have a friend help or hire a professional.[9]

Related to lead magnets, I should discuss the concept of *calls to action*. The call to action is the one thing you want readers of your website to do when they first arrive on the homepage. Donald Miller writes and speaks about this in simple and helpful ways.[10] Most websites, he argues, are too cluttered; readers don't know what they are supposed to do when they arrive. A clear call to action guides readers. Ideally, the call to action should be coupled with the lead magnet to solve a problem readers have. Typical calls to

[9] If you create an ebook from your blog post inventory, please take great care to expunge the residue that identifies the content as being former blog posts. So, if a blog post had a line that said, "In this *post* I want to tell you about . . . ," instead write, "In this *ebook* I want to tell you about . . . ." This particular example sentence reads fairly inelegantly either way, but you get the idea. Failing to make these changes will cheapen the reading experience, even if the reader already knew the ebook came from posts.

[10] Donald Miller, *Building a StoryBrand*, 24–25, 145–56.

action include "subscribe," "read recent posts," or "buy my book"—but these are generally weak calls to action because they do not solve a problem the reader has. For example, you may want visitors to subscribe to your blog. Fine, but just because you want readers to subscribe, doesn't mean website visitors want to subscribe. You need to connect subscribing to your blog with a solution to a problem.

I'll give a better example than "subscribe." Perhaps in large letters at the top of your homepage you write,

There's too much angry banter in the Christian world.

Then, right under this line you could write something like,

*Subscribe to read articles about what unites us
    rather than what divides.*

The picture you place in the background might be of someone reading on a tablet who looks happy. I'm just making this up, so you can probably do better. Miller says every visitor to your website should be able to scan the homepage in a few seconds and know (1) What do you offer? (2) How will it make my life better? (3) What do I need to do to buy it [or subscribe]?[11] He calls this *passing the grunt test*, meaning "a caveman could look at your website and immediately grunt what you offer."[12]

My example about angry banter and Christian unity is too wordy to be skimmed quickly by a first-time website visitor. But hopefully my example illustrates how "subscribing" (the call to action) is best paired with a theme in your writing

[11] Ibid, 24.
[12] Ibid.

(e.g., unity in Christ), which is cast as a solution to a problem (e.g., angry disunity in the Christian world).

Add your call to action and lead magnet "above the fold" of the homepage. The fold is a newspaper term, meaning the top half of the newspaper that can be read without opening the paper. On a website, above the fold means what a reader can see without scrolling. Make sure your above-the-fold homepage can pass the grunt test. If you have older posts that generate search engine traffic, you can retrofit those to have the same general lead magnet as the rest of the website, or perhaps one more tailored to the post. In either case, you'll have to decide whether a call to action at the top is too aggressive or if it fits better at the bottom of the post.

> When I began blogging, I didn't know what a blessing it would be in my life and how it would help me sort and process my experiences through spiritual eyes. I could have used more of that in my twenties. Blogging helps me think, process, and be on the lookout for the Holy Spirit's work in the world around me. – *Melissa Edgington,* <u>*yourmomhasablog.com*</u>

Finally, consider adding a pop-up call to action on your blog. Yes, pop-ups are annoying, but they still tend to be a useful tool in growing email lists, which helps the blogger, of course, but also serves readers by connecting them to a website and author that they, ostensibly, appreciated. To make pop-ups less obtrusive, you can adjust the settings so that they only appear if a visitor scrolls to the middle or bottom of a post or after remaining on the site for a set amount of time, like ten or thirty seconds. Pop-ups also use *web cookies* to know who has previously visited a website and thus who doesn't need to be shown the same pop-up again and again. Web cookies are the little bits of data that a website stores on a user's computer while the user is browsing the site.

Website logins, for example, use cookies to remember usernames and passwords.[13]

Marketing to the Glory of God

Before moving to the next section, permit a brief word about the goodness of marketing. At my church right now I'm attempting to solve a problem we have with online giving. The system we use has proven frustrating. I have done some research, but other demands of pastoring have taken priority. When I stumble upon a website of a company who offers these services, I need to quickly assess the specifics of what they do, how to get signed up, and how much their services cost. In short, I need someone to market to me; it's the only way I will solve our church's giving problem without wasting more of our God-given resources.

Of course, I could add descriptive words to that statement, so that it reads something like, "I need someone to market to me in a non-greasy and truthful way," but those additions are unnecessary, or they should be. When a company takes the time and effort to develop a quality product and they know how it might help others, sharing that information in clear and compelling ways, they are marketing. And that's an honorable endeavor.

So it is with your blog. Sure, you could put a banner at the top of your homepage that says you expect every visitor to read fifteen of your posts, notice the themes you commonly explore, the depth of analysis you provide, the strength of your facility with the craft, your theological moorings, and how all of that will help the reader in her life situation. But that asks a lot of readers and it's not the kind of blogging that

---

[13] Public service announcement: clearing your cookies is not the same as woofing.

does unto others what you would want done unto you. It's also not the way Paul modeled sharing the gospel. "We have renounced disgraceful, underhanded ways," he writes. Instead, "by the open statement of the truth we would commend ourselves to everyone's conscience in the sight of God" (2 Cor 4:2). Paul found a way to forsake the underbelly often associated with promotion, yet he still succinctly shared the message of hope in Christ. Therefore, your pop-up windows, calls to action, email lists, and the like *could* all be marshaled in the promotion of self but are first and better understood as the outworking of love and compassion for readers. When companies who sell online giving services market in this way—renouncing underhanded ways and offering open statements of truth—churches are served. And when bloggers market in this way, readers are served and God's glory is upheld.

Pictures, with Thoughts on Stealing and Plagiarism

Now that we've set up our website, email lists, and marketing, we turn our attention to the visual appeal. Compelling pictures enhance your beautifully written blog posts the way the perfect coffee mug makes drinking coffee more enjoyable. The mug is not the content; the coffee is. But the mug keeps the coffee warm and makes you feel good as you hold it. Photography is similar; it's not the content, but well-chosen photos make reading more enjoyable. The numbers back this up. One expert notes, "Articles with relevant images get 94% more page views and 50% more shares than pages without images."[14] As you select pictures, try to avoid "picture clichés" as you would "writing clichés." For

---

[14] Dani Stewart, "How to Create a Visual Identity for Your Blog," *Tradecraft*, no. 3 (2017): 31.

example, in a post about blogging, avoid pictures that feature an Apple laptop next to local brew latte art. Clever pairing of pictures and words becomes difficult because stock photography drifts toward standard tropes, even becoming memes, such as those woman-laughing-alone-with-salad photos, a picture cliché you'll certainly want to avoid.[15]

You can buy photos on various websites, which works fine if your business makes enough money to justify buying images. But most of us are not making that kind of money. I never spend money on photography. My current favorite place to get free photography is Unsplash.com.[16] Be careful using free photos, though. You have to read the fine print about when and where photos can be used without cost. Some photos are free to use so long as you give proper attribution. Some photos are free so long as you are not using them to sell a product, like putting the photo on the cover of a book. Others are free so long as you don't modify them. Others are free without any restrictions on usage.

> The most unexpected thing I've learned from blogging is how much titles and images matter. You can write the most profound blog post on a particular topic, but if your title and image are bad, few people will read.
> – Chris Martin, *chrismartin.blog*

If your method for finding photos involves doing a Google search for an image, saving the file to your computer, and uploading it to an article, you're probably stealing. Take this seriously. Using stolen pictures undermines blogging for God's glory. You don't want people plagiarizing your words, so don't plagiarize someone's photos.

---

[15] Google that salad one; it's a thing.
[16] Other helpful sources for free pictures include pexels.com and creativecommons.org.

Be aware that search engines cannot read images; they read the alt-text, which comes from metadata, all the identifying information about a website or post, such as author, date, and keywords. So as you insert pictures into your posts, be sure to include helpful titles for pictures.

Miscellaneous Tech Topics

We've hit the big topics related to the technical side of blogging, but several smaller yet still important topics remain. I'll go more quickly as we finish out the chapter, giving some topics a few sentences and others a few short paragraphs.

Real Simple Syndication (RSS)

RSS stands for Real Simple Syndication. An *RSS feed* allows users to subscribe to internet content (typically blogs, vlogs, and podcasts) from specific websites and have the website's content curated and delivered. An *RSS Aggregator* is software used to read *RSS feeds*. For those who read a lot of blogs, an RSS feed keeps curated content in one place. A quick search through the Help section of your blogging platform should help you confirm your RSS feed is working properly.

Hyperlinking and 404 Page

Most blog posts have one, or even several, embedded hyperlinks or just links for short. Adding links is the online way of footnoting your sources. When you link away from your site to elsewhere on the internet, make the setting of the link set to "open in a new window." You had to work hard to get that visitor; don't send him away without offering an easy way back. Generally, links within your website from one place to another should just open without opening a new window.

For various reasons, a link may become broken. Broken links are links that no longer direct users to active webpages and instead return an error message. If the broken link is an internal link on your website, it will take visitors to your 404 page, an error message page that web designers can control. If the broken link is an external link, it will take visitors to that website's 404 page, unless the whole website is defunct, in which case the user will receive some other error message. To check a website's 404 page, add "/404.php" after the domain name (e.g., benjaminvrbicek.com/404.php).

> If you have a blog read by only a few dozen readers, you're making a bigger impact than you probably realize. With fifty people reading your blog, you have more people in your "classroom" than most professors at Harvard. With ninety readers, you have more in your "pews" than most pastors have in their churches. And with a thousand readers, you have a larger "circulation" than most poetry and short story magazines. Too many bloggers scorn their influence because they aren't reaching stadiums full of people. – *Joe Carter,* *thegospelcoalition.org*

Categories and Tags

Blogging effectively entails learning the difference between categories and tags. A category is a group of similar content under one name or phrase. Each blog post is typically marked in one or more categories to help readers find similar posts, for example, the category of "Book Reviews," "Preaching," or "Blogging." Categories are broader than tags, which tend to be very specific. Think about tags like the index at the back of a book. If the post were a book, and something in the post would be helpful to be identified in an index, then it should be listed as a tag. Common tags are author names, cultural events, books of the Bible, theological terms, and keywords. Tags are considered part of a blog post's metadata, along with category, author, date, and other items.[17] Although you see them less frequently today, for many years fashionable blogs had a *cloud tag*, a visual representation of all of the tags used on a blog. Often the words used more frequently appear larger.

Search Engine Optimization (SEO)

People have written books about search engine optimization, but the basic idea involves creating content that is more likely to be found by internet searches.[18] Sometimes, bloggers even work backward, noting what people are already searching for on the internet and then writing content tailored to those searches. Optimizing a post for search engines means considering length, linking, metadata, and using keywords. Keywords are the words that people commonly use in searches. Keywords can be either *short-tail* or *long-tail*, with the latter being more specific. A short-tail keyword might be "God's promises," and a long-tail version could be "God's promises when you have cancer."[19]

---

[17] Tags also help search engine optimization, so, in addition to the typical tags of names, books, and themes, creating tags with short phrases and questions (e.g., "how to read my Bible when I'm tired") seems to help posts rank higher in search engines.

[18] For a good primer on SEO, see the entire May 2018 issue of ConvertKit's magazine *Tradecraft* ("Learn SEO Strategy for Creators: Get More than Website Traffic," *Tradecraft*, no. 17 [2018]).

[19] One website suggests that when "going through your past content and auditing it, ask yourself, 'What keyword is this post even targeting? Is it optimized enough?'" To be candid, that is work I'll never do—not as I audit old posts and only in the most minor ways as I write new ones. My literary bent won't let me clutter prose so arbitrarily. I write to be read, not

By typing short-tail keywords into Google's search bar, the self-populating suggestion feature will show you common searches. For example, when I typed, "God's promises when," the search bar suggested, ". . . you are hurting," ". . . you are discouraged," and other slight variants. Including these phrases in your post, especially the title, will improve your Google ranking.

Google Ads (formerly Google Adwords) allows you to buy the ability to rank at the top of Google search results. You have likely seen these ads, even if you didn't know you were looking at paid advertising. In many Google searches, the top one or two sites listed have the word "Ad" right before their web address and description. The person or company who bought that ad space only pays when visitors click the promoted link, which is called pay-per-click (PPC). When promoting your website or a specific post with Google Ads, popular keywords can be competitive, which means they cost more to rank near the top. Because long-tail keywords are more specific, they tend to be less competitive and thus cost less. Google Ads are created in monthly campaigns where you set a defined budget. You can tweak or abandon the ad at any time during the campaign.[20]

Google Analytics

Google Analytics is a robust tool for tracking statistics about visitors to your website. Common blogging metrics

---

skimmed by people or bots. But then again, maybe I should try harder at SEO; the title of the post comes from a website boasting four hundred thousand visits a month, and I have four thousand. ("45 Things I Wish I Knew Before Starting a Blog That Gets 400,000 Visits/m," *CodeInWP.com*, May 7, 2020, https://www.codeinwp.com/blog/starting-a-blog/.)

[20] There is a difference between Google Ads and Google Adsense. Google Ads allows you to advertise on the Google search results pages, while Adsense is the platform to display Google Ads on your website.

include pageviews, blog comments, and social media shares, but Google Analytics provides way more than these, with stats such as bounce rate, site speed, and conversions. These might sound like techno-babble to some of you, as much of what Google Analytics offers remains helpful only to the professional blogger.

To set up Google Analytics, create an account and install the tracking ID into your website code. This step might require you to consult a tutorial specific to your blogging platform, but because this is such a common activity, there will surely be several. I would encourage you to install this tracking tool even if you do not plan on using it presently. Having Google Analytics set up is like drawing lines on the door jamb as your kids grow taller. It's nice to have years later, but you can't have it then if you don't get it set up now.

> Honesty and vulnerability—admitting that you don't know something—is a surprisingly rich way to generate authentic engagement with readers, perhaps because it's so rarely seen in the egocentric Wild West of the world wide web.
> – Abby Farson Pratt, abbyfp.com

Spend What You Can

We have defined blogging for God's glory as having our motivations aligned with God's and also pursuing excellence in the craft, which includes theological precision, beautiful prose, visual appeal, and the edification of readers, all drawing from the best industry practices. I do not want to imply that *excellence* must always also mean *expensive* or *extravagant*. If you can only afford a free WordPress website, your blog can still glorify God, just as an ordinary church building constructed and maintained with excellence can glorify God.

You don't need the blogging equivalent of an ornate cathedral. And as I mentioned at the start of this chapter, while I can never go back in time to upgrade the quality of my wedding video, bloggers can always upgrade their websites in the future.

Yet with these principles understood, I would recommend that *if* you can afford expenses to your blog, spend more. The extra investment will help keep you motivated—you've got skin in the game. Because blogs have become so prevalent, spending a bit more will help you stand out from the crowd. Additionally and most importantly, there is a cumulative witness to God's glory when Christian bloggers do all that we can to pursue excellence, not for the sake of our name among the nations but for the sake of God's.

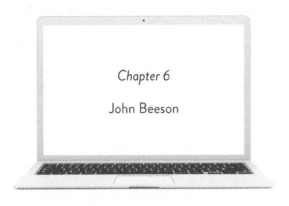

Chapter 6

John Beeson

NETWORKING

How Will I Connect with Readers and Like-Minded Bloggers?

Y ou've met the type: they wear a little too much cologne, lean in a little too close for comfort, act like you're old friends when you've only just met, and it's only a matter of time until the business card comes out. The networker.

I have an allergy to networking. Business meetups, conferences, and even the exchange of business cards have always made me uncomfortable. In fact, I don't believe I've ever re-ordered business cards. And yet, strangely, I've realized that just four years into my time in Tucson I've become a well-connected pastor in the area. I've become a networker. Oh no. What gives?

Networking at its worst is the contemporary manifestation of the Tower of Babel, each participant maneuvering to make a name for himself with individuals used as human stepping-stones to the top of the tower.

But networking (or use the word connecting, if you

prefer) is redeemable. Like anything we do, our motives are critical to whether our work glorifies God or ourselves. I realized early into my ministry in Tucson that many pastors are islands—disconnected from the city church. If I reached out to some of these pastors to hear their stories and offer encouragement and prayer, bridges would be forged connecting the islands. I became convicted that one of the most selfless things I could do in my ministry was the ministry of networking.

Believe in Your Calling

If you want to write to serve yourself then you should journal. Journaling is a healthy spiritual discipline. I'm grateful for its presence in my life. But if you want to write to serve others, you need to network in the service of your blog. You need to network for the service of God.

I love how Kate Motaung and Shannon Popkin reflect on the relationship between author and reader in their book *Influence*: "I've discovered that it's not about how high I can climb on the ladder of man-made success. It's about how I can offer myself as a means for others to climb the ladder toward eternity with Christ."[1] If you truly are offering yourself as a ladder "toward eternity with Christ," there is no reason to shy away from being bold.

When I first launched my blog I posted a link on my Facebook account encouraging my friends to subscribe if they were interested, and I emailed several friends and congregants to ask if they might be interested. I had a number of people sign up initially, and that was that. I was encouraged

---

[1] Kate Motaung and Shannon Popkin, *Influence: Building a Platform that Elevates Jesus (Not Me)* (Independently Published, 2018), 94.

by my start. I hoped that this core group would help raise a flag for me. Hoping others would take it from there, I didn't do any further promotion for over a year. But the cavalry never arrived. My numbers stalled out and then dropped off.

A year later I was disappointed and frustrated with the lack of traction. My wife helped me sort out some sin in my heart: ingratitude and pride, to name two. But she also helped me clarify the question of where I wanted my blog to go next. Since my blog launched, Facebook had become significantly less blog-friendly, all but locking down the visibility of my posts to the majority of Facebook friends. If I wanted more people to see my blog, I was going to have to do that work myself, not just expect it to happen on its own.

Because of these conversations I was able to clarify my original blogging commitment: to benefit the people of our church. I was convinced my ministry of blogging was benefiting the church. Stories trickled back to me of those who had been encouraged and challenged by my posts. I believed there was an incremental and snowballing discipleship impact that was being felt at New Life. If I thought the blog was a benefit to others, neglecting to promote it was actually an act of pride, not humility. And so, I pulled up the list of our attenders and composed an email with a sample post inviting them to subscribe. I prayed that God would lead some to respond whose discipleship would be strengthened by the blog. And sure enough, many did.

Meanwhile, I began to spend some time crafting posts for websites with a broader readership. My purpose in this was a heart of stewarding my gifting for the broader church. I realized that this broader and larger audience was not my first or even ultimate target, but that there was work I was doing that could be repurposed to serve this audience. If I could benefit them, I wanted to be able to do so.

Serving Other Readers and Bloggers

If this is all about the reader, you also should consider whether you want to submit guest posts. I wouldn't recommend doing this too early. You'll want to build a strong foundation for your blog before cantilevering to a broader audience. Then consider which websites would be a good match for you. Don't necessarily look for the biggest sites. A great fit might be another smaller site. But neither should you discount your ability to serve the audience of a larger site. Determine if you can curate what you write for those websites so they best fit the crossover between your brand and their brand.

Perhaps you are noticing that some of your content would benefit a larger audience. Look into the best way to make connections with those who run the sites. Many authors and editors are very accessible, whether via Twitter or their website. Make sure you follow the submissions process, if it is posted. Do unto other authors as you would want them to do unto you. If you appreciate a post, let them know and share it. Be a raving fan of others before you expect raving fans of your own. Be generous in celebrating others. Kate Motaung and Shannon Popkin encourage writers to "highlight the accomplishments and achievements of other brothers and sisters in Christ when you notice jobs well done. Leave encouraging comments on blog posts or articles that you read. Share quotes from your favorite books or articles on Twitter, Instagram, or Facebook."[2] Lifting up others is what Christians do.

A heart check is in order. This isn't advice on how to "make friends and influence people"; it's advice on how to treat others well. It's important to check your motives on this front. Protect your expectations as well. Will everyone respond as you reach out? Of course not. There are plenty of bloggers who are pretty insulated and inaccessible, but there are a lot more than you would think who respond if you reach out.

When you reach out to a site that allows guest posts, do your homework. Get to know the site, the tone, and the audience. If you are able to establish a relationship with the author or website editor first, that is ideal. A cold email, just like a cold call, is the least likely to get the desired response. When you reach out, do so humbly. Introduce yourself, express your appreciation for the site, and simply explain why you think the post might be a good fit for their site.

You might want to consider asking friends who are gifted writers to help you edit your posts. This requires time and planning on the part of the blogger. So if you typically publish the way most bloggers do, leaving little time between writing and publishing,[3] you'll struggle to give editors the time they need to help, especially if they are volunteers. But this step is crucial to improving your posts. This breathing room also protects you from responding to current issues without careful thought. Sleeping on a post and hearing the counsel of others is the path of wisdom. Justin Taylor, a

---

[2] Motaung and Popkin, *Influence*, 102.

[3] "According to our survey, 52% of bloggers write either the day before or on the same day as they plan to publish," (Dani Stewart, "How to Create a Year-Long Content Strategy," *Tradecraft*, no. 3 [2017]: 21).

pioneer in evangelical blogging, said he's learned "that instantaneous response is not necessarily the path of a virtuous response."[4]

One of the most important partnerships I have is with my editing team. I have eight or so people who are gracious enough to read and edit my posts before they go up. They are helpful to me for at least two reasons. First, they help catch typos, and second, they help provide early feedback regarding the tone and content of my posts. I'm grateful this team catches when I am unclear or overly critical. They also help generate ideas, and, as excellent writers in their own right, they have an open invitation to provide contributions to my blog themselves.

Caring for Your Readers

Cultivate relationships not only with other bloggers but also with your readers. My readers have provided great suggestions for topics they would like to see me cover. They have been generous enough to share posts with their friends, interact with posts, ask great questions, and provide insightful feedback. The best blogs are relational—the author with the readers, the readers with the author, and the readers with other readers. The more you know your readers and are available to them, the more invested they will be in your blog. This is why I have a very open platform. I allow comments and rarely delete them on my blog or under Facebook posts. I also provide my contact information. This doesn't mean every negative comment demands your attention and

---

[4] Joe Carter, "The Class of 2003: An Interview with Justin Taylor," *The Gospel Coalition*, October 22, 2013, https://www.thegospelcoalition.org/article/the-class-of-2003-an-interview-with-justin-taylor/.

response. We know how deflating they can be. Even seven years ago Jared C. Wilson noted the toxicity of blog comments, saying comment threads have "become this veritable graffiti wall where drive-by malcontents can fling their poo like monkeys."[5] Knowing that I have glorified God lessens the sting when the poo gets flung in my direction.

Each blogger has to have his or her own set of internal guidelines. My tendency errs on the side of over-accessibility. The purpose of my blog is pastoral in nature, and so I want my availability to match the blog's tone. I've found that private messaging with critics is a much more productive way of handling conflict than public responses. To that end, I usually don't provide a lengthy response to public criticism unless the criticism is asking for a clarification that I didn't make in the post itself. To repeat the counter-assertion often proves unhelpful. You're just dealing with someone who disagrees with you. And, of course, there will always be those who disagree. That's not a reason to be upset. It can take up a fair amount of mental and emotional energy, though, and you have to be prepared for this.

It will be helpful from the beginning to define how and when you might be willing to post others' material on your blog. Do you want to solicit friends to write posts for you? What will your vetting guidelines be for posts sent to you? Will you have the submission requirements posted on your website, or will that be done through private channels of communication? How can you be sure to steward your readers' time and the tone of your blog? More open policies of sharing posts can have their benefits: when you post others'

---

[5] Joe Carter, "The Class of 2003: An Interview with Jared Wilson," *The Gospel Coalition*, October 21, 2013, https://www.thegospelcoalition.org/article/the-class-of-2003-an-interview-with-jared-wilson/.

work on your blog, they're likely to share it themselves. But a more closed policy has the benefit of protecting your blog's brand and quality. I don't state on my site that I take outside contributions, but I'm very open to private inquiries. You'll want to create a policy that best fits your purposes.

A Naturally Lonely Calling

Blogging can be an isolated calling. Do everything you can to remain in community. Encourage other bloggers, and be real enough to experience the encouragement that can come from those in the trenches with you.

While blogging may be lonely, remember you weren't made to blog alone any more than you were made to serve God in any capacity alone. You were made for community. I love the intimacy of Paul's request for Timothy and Mark to visit him in prison at the close of 2 Timothy. Paul says, "Do your best to come to me soon. For Demas, in love with this present world, has deserted me and gone to Thessalonica, Crescens has gone to Galatia, Titus to Dalmatia. Luke alone is with me. Get Mark and bring him with you, for he is very useful to me for ministry" (2 Tim 4:9–11). Can you hear the yearning of Paul's heart in that passage? He is lonely. And he knows that he is better when his friends surround him.

> I'm never really writing in isolation. Through social media, writers groups, and private messages or emails, I've developed friendships with other writers who are continually refining me. Blogging is a conversation; I'm not just shouting into a void. – *Cassie Watson*, **casswatson.com**

You will be a better writer when you write in community. You will be a smarter blogger when you blog alongside others. I'm so impressed with bloggers such as Chris Thomas (ploughmansrest.com), who offers himself as a guide and pours engagement into other bloggers. Something that started as a small Slack channel with the intent to build up other writers has grown into a large group hosted by Gospel-Centered Discipleship.[6] Tim Challies consistently points his massive readership to bloggers with much smaller audiences.

Paul, the Networker

Without a doubt, Paul was a networker. Flip open Paul's letters, and you'll find him close by greeting those in the church by name. In the pastoral epistles alone Paul mentions thirty-four individuals. In Romans, even though Paul is writing to a church he's never visited, he builds a relational bridge with the church through the mutual relationships they share. In the final chapter he mentions thirty-four more by name.

Paul offers his good name to friends who could use it. He leverages the respect he has earned in churches for the sake of others. In 1 Corinthians he closes with this admonition: "When Timothy comes, see that you put him at ease among you, for he is doing the work of the Lord, as I am. So let no one despise him. Help him on his way in peace, that he may return to me, for I am expecting him with the brothers" (1 Cor 16:10–11). He then goes on to praise "the household of Stephanas" and urges the church to "be subject to such as these, and to every fellow worker and laborer" (1 Cor 16:16). He closes his letter to the Ephesians by building up the carrier of the letter, Tychicus, and informing the church

[6] I encourage you to consider joining the group: https://gcdiscipleship.com/writers-guild.

of the purpose of Tychicus's ministry among them (Eph 6:21–22). Paul does likewise in Colossians (Col 4:7–9).

Clearly, Paul sees his network of relationships as an asset to his ministry, and he is quick to bless others in his network. Don't shy away from what Paul leans into. Any influence God has given you, he invites you to share. The path to humility is not to withdraw from relationships but to build others up in the context of relationship.

Would you pray right now for other bloggers God would allow to cross your path? If an author's writing has blessed you, how could you encourage him or her? What is one tangible way you could help another writer? Just this morning a friend of mine from seminary who just had his first book published reached out to me thanking me for my encouragement in his life. We caught up with one another, and he offered to introduce me to some publishing contacts. How generous is that? Who might God be calling me to serve in a similar fashion today?

Your blogging ministry will last longer and your impact will reach further if you partner with others.

Before I started my blog, I reached out to Benjamin for his advice. He was generous enough to spend several hours corresponding with me and talking with me on the phone as he helped me learn from his hard-earned lessons. Benjamin wasn't just at the starting line with me; he has been a friend through the whole journey. We've celebrated each other's successes; we've empathized with one another over disappointments. We've given each other feedback and have brought invaluable perspective from the outside. I'm so grateful for Benjamin's friendship, encouragement, and sharpening. I hope you are blessed to have a fellow blogger like Benjamin in your life as well.

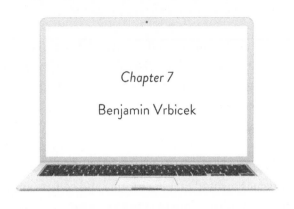

SUCCESS

How Do Bloggers Make Money, and What Even Defines "Winning"?

T hus far we've only discussed ways to spend money on a blog, but before we end the book we want to also discuss ways to make money while blogging. Many Christians, however, get uncomfortable when talking about money, as though making any money equals the desire to swan dive into a sea of cash like Scrooge McDuck. This discomfort around money is even more present among Christian artists because of the stigma that exists more broadly between art and money. On top of all this, additional complexity results because the hearts of all are prone to store up treasure on earth, which the Scriptures repeatedly warn against (e.g., Matt 6:19–21).

However, it's *the love* of money that is the root of all evil, not the making of money (1 Tim 6:10). If you labor at something for the glory of God and the good of others, there is nothing inherently wrong with making income from your labors. Jesus and Paul remind us that the worker deserves his wages (Luke 10:7; 1 Tim 5:18). As much as I want to keep my heart from making money into an idol, sometimes the pushback among Christians needs to go in the other direction—making money is not only okay, but it could even be a good thing.

In a blog post on her website, Jen Pollock Michel wrestles with the issues around making money and self-promotion as an author. The post comes from a series of back-and-forth letters she wrote with author Shawn Smucker.

> I'd love to get your thoughts on something that I recently saw on social media. A husband of someone who had recently published a book posted this: "My wife is far too classy and has more important things to say than to use her platform to constantly try and sell her books. I however, have no class and nothing better to say. I apologize in advance for the next few months (year?). ORDER HER BOOK HERE." The insinuation was so familiar, so awful. It's this idea that there's something suspicious, if not sleazy, about working hard to sell your books. It's this assumption that the angels among us don't have to. These tight-lipped saints choose the moral high road— in this case, silence about the books they publish—and their books grow wings and fly into the hands of paying customers.
>
> Now don't get me wrong. I'm as annoyed as anyone else by those authors that think their books are God's gift to the world's readership, authors who are disappointed when their first book doesn't win a major prize or make a bestseller list. I have no patience for self-importance. We as writers have to learn something about the

modesty of faithfulness. We might do what God calls us to do, and our impact might be the slightest ripple on the smallest pond.

But here's the truth we both know: you and I can't keep writing books if we can't sell the books we've already written. This is the cold reality of publishing. We can't simply do this for fun or even for our own formation. If we want to write for readers, then we're going to need them to know about our books. We're going to need them to buy them. This doesn't mean, of course, that you and I have to hawk copies from the trunk of our cars in the church parking lot, but it does mean we can't keep this work a secret.[1]

I love her line about those authors who seem above having to sell their books because "their books grow wings and fly into the hands of paying customers." I realize the main concern in this chapter relates to making money on a blog, not specifically selling books, but I think her reflections apply to both. Michel apprises the dangers of both over- and under-promotion, while maintaining the goodness of promoting, even for an income. This tension between over- and under-promotion can feel like walking a razor's edge, but I'd encourage you to see the path is wider than we often think.

Four Ways to Make Money

As you develop your blog, there are four main ways to make money, or *monetize* your blog, as it's often called. You can court patrons, establish affiliate partnerships, offer

---

[1] Jen Pollock Michel, "Postmarked: Dear Shawn (15)," November 8, 2019, https://www.jenpollockmichel.com/blog/2019/11/7/postmarked-dear-shawn-15.

advertising, and sell products. No single way is better than the others, and likely many bloggers try them all.

Court Patrons

I know raising money isn't exactly the same thing as making money. But that's what this first strategy is. You ask people who benefit from your writing to support your writing. Jesus certainly had those who supported his ministry. Luke records that as Jesus was "proclaiming and bringing the good news of the kingdom of God," he also traveled with his twelve disciples, others he had healed, and "Joanna, the wife of Chuza, Herod's household manager, and Susanna, and many others, *who provided for them out of their means*" (Luke 8:1–3, emphasis added).

Speaking of Luke, he likely had a patron who bankrolled his travel for eyewitness interviews and the purchasing of expensive writing supplies. Some biblical scholars believe it was Theophilus, the man to whom he addressed each volume (Luke 1:1–4; Acts 1:1–3). When talking about generous patrons of ministry, the apostle Paul's friend Phoebe also comes to mind. In Romans 16 he calls her a sister and servant of the church and urges the church in Rome to "welcome her in the Lord in a way worthy of the saints, and help her in whatever she may need from you." Paul gives this instruction because, he says, "she has been a patron of many and of myself as well" (Rom 16:1–2).

If asking for money makes you uneasy, keep in mind that you are not so much asking for money as inviting people to partner with you in a worthy ministry. This is how support-raising missionaries and parachurch workers view raising funds.

You can ask for money in several ways. You can ask with focused, personal requests to people who know you and benefit from your writing ministry. You can ask for money by making general requests through periodic blog posts. And you can ask for money passively by leaving a place on your website for people to donate. I've tried all three: targeted, focused, and passive requests. At the bottom of my About Page, I have this note:

> *How can you help?* It takes a lot of time to keep this blog burning but actually not all that much money. Really, it just takes a few dollars each month to purchase web hosting, books, editing, and maybe a few cups of coffee. If you like what you read, and think others would too, perhaps you'd like to toss a log on the fire. I would greatly appreciate it.

Thus far almost no one has given via my donation button. It's been a sweet surprise when my inbox receives a notification that someone did. But now that this verbiage is in print in this book, maybe I'll start practicing my McDuck swan dive.

Establish Affiliate Partnerships

Right below this donation paragraph on my website I have another short statement about a different way I've tried to make money on my website. Affiliate partnerships are relationships with other businesses that are mutually beneficial; as you help out a business, they give you something in return. The Amazon Affiliate Program is the most common affiliate program for bloggers. (Target, Best Buy, and many other companies have similar programs.) The

Amazon Affiliate Program works with most but not all blogging platforms (e.g., WordPress.org, not WordPress.com). When bloggers send readers to Amazon's website via a link with your website's unique fingerprint in the URL, and those readers buy something from Amazon, affiliate partners get a small commission from the purchase, a kickback if you will.

Let me use an example. The link below will take you to the Amazon page of Tony Reinke's book *12 Ways Your Phone Is Changing You*:

    amazon.com/dp/1433552434

When you click the Amazon link on Desiring God's website about the book, the link's URL looks similar but slightly longer:

    amazon.com/dp/1433552434/?desigod06-20

When I reviewed Reinke's book on my blog, I also included an Amazon link, which should look similar to the second, longer URL at Desiring God:

    amazon.com/dp/1433552434/?faf0e-20

I doubt many readers look closely at URLs, but the longer links indicate that we both participate in the Amazon Affiliate Program. On the Desiring God website you can find a statement about this.

> Desiring God is a participant in the Amazon Services LLC Associates Program, an affiliate advertising program designed to provide a means for sites to earn advertising fees by advertising and linking to Amazon.com.

You can find a similar statement on my website. In fact, Amazon requires that participants in their affiliate program disclose their participation.

For me, the Amazon Affiliate Program hasn't been the cash cow I anticipated. I just jumped over to Amazon and looked at my earnings report for the last thirty days. I've made a whopping $0.24. Other months I've done better, but in the previous four years I've still only totaled $38.66. I suppose if I blogged about photography and reviewed high-end cameras, the clicks over to Amazon and subsequent purchases might generate more lucrative commissions.

An additional factor works against bloggers in trying to monetize through Amazon's Affiliate Program. Amazon does not include commissions from purchases made by friends and family. Because this is proprietary information, Amazon does not disclose how they determine who your friends and family are, though it is likely based on your social media accounts. For this reason, the vast majority of purchases made via Amazon through links do not earn any profits for John and me.

Offer Advertising

Selling advertising spots on your website is another way to make money. This is fairly straightforward, so I won't give much explanation. I will, however, offer a caution. You can sell ad space to specific companies with specific products, and you can sell general ad space to marketing companies who then fill that ad space with seemingly random products. General advertising means you don't know which specific product will be advertised. This can sometimes be a problem for those who seek to honor God with their blog. More than a few times I've read blog posts by Christians while seeing ads littered throughout the post that, I assume, the author would not endorse. Before you sell general advertising on your website, read the fine print carefully.

Sell Products

The final way to make money is selling products, such as books, courses, coaching, or any other product you might desire to sell. If you do this, make sure you use a blogging platform that makes the process smooth for both buyer and seller. Pastor and author Carey Nieuwhof does this well, offering a number of different courses on his website.

Be Realistic about Growth and Making Money

All things being equal, I'd prefer to make money with my blog than lose money. There's nothing too controversial about that, right? You would rather *earn* $100 than *spend* $100, and so would I.

Beware, though, of the stories of seemingly overnight success that plague the blogging world. These stories can be encouraging, but they also tend to stir discontentment and unrealistic expectations. I love what popular blogger Jeff Goins has said: "The truth is there is no such thing as overnight success. Or if there is, it never happens overnight."[2] That encourages me.

But his website has a way of discouraging me too. When you visit, a pop-up welcomes you with the promise:

[2] Jeff Goins, "058: Launching a Blockbuster Blog on a Budget: Interview with Ruth Soukup," *The Portfolio Life*, https://goinswriter.com/ruth-soukup/ and on Twitter, June 3, 2015, 9:00 p.m., https://twitter.com/JeffGoins/status/606264250349273088.

100K Readers in 18 Months? Yes, it's possible. Learn how in my free guide.

I've found most of Goins's writings and podcasts encouraging and helpful, but this statement feels like unrealistic propaganda. Is getting 100K readers in just eighteen months possible? *Yes.* But probable? *No.* Goins's own success involves years and years of blogging unsuccessfully. In fact, when you learn more of the details, he started and ended eight blogs before the ninth one reached all those subscribers in eighteen months. These sorts of promises abound in blogging books and posts. In *Make Money from Blogging*, Lisa Tanner and Sally Miller write, "After one year (assuming you're consistent and have a message people want to hear) you can earn anywhere from $1,000 a month to six figures a year."[3] I suppose a person *could* do that. But again, is it probable? No. I pick on this excerpt because the section header asks, "Why Start a Blog?" and the first sentence asks, "What can you reasonably expect after blogging for a year?"[4] The "go and do likewise" implication is unreasonable.

> We have enough triumphalist, "how to succeed in ministry" blogs. When I read blogs, I'm looking for encouragement and hope for simply getting out of bed tomorrow and faithfully following Jesus till I rest my head the following night. – *Chris Thomas, ploughmansrest.com*

So much of the blogging influencer subculture is one giant, cannibalistic pyramid scheme that one ascends by teaching others how to ascend as they have. A few pages later, the same book tells of a blogger who began blogging

---

[3] Lisa Tanner and Sally Miller, *Make Money from Blogging: How to Start a Blog While Raising a Family* (Independently Published, 2018), 11.
[4] Ibid.

with one theme but later realized her "true passion was helping other moms create profitable blogs. She made the switch and her blog and profits soared."[5] This is what I mean by cannibalism: you eat others to grow. There are exceptions, of course. I've sat through webinars where I swelled with thanksgiving over the host's generous and thoughtful sharing of resources on how to grow my platform and increase my blogging effectiveness. I've also sat in webinars that made me want to barf.

So, whether you have ten subscribers or ten thousand, and whether you make money or lose money, commit yourself now to blog for God's glory, using the best blogging practices you can while letting God be the one who brings the growth.

How Do Bloggers Define "Hitting It Big"?

Christian ministry seems to struggle with the right metrics for measuring success. Some metrics are easy to count, so we tend to count them. For example, we give the prefix *mega* to any church with over two thousand regular attendees. Attendees are easy to count. Perhaps all bloggers would be helped if we gave the objective epithet *megablog* to any blog with two thousand regular readers.

But the question of how online writers measure success—whether in terms of pageviews, engagement, subscribers, products sold, or something else—should also cause us to dig deeper, to excavate the struggles related to success buried in our hearts. How do we define hitting it big? How do we know when we've been successful?

[5] Ibid., 16–17.

Relationships with Publishers or Lots of Web Traffic? Or Something Else?

J. A. Medders and Chase Replogle both interviewed pastor and author Scott Sauls on their writing podcasts.[6] In these interviews Sauls detailed his resistance to authorship despite publishers courting him for years to write a book. I don't know if the courting from publishers happened because of his blogging, his pastoring and church planting, his networking, or all of these together. To me, having publishers knocking on your door is big time. This is not to discount the work Sauls eventually had to do to write proposals and complete manuscripts (I assume he did still have to write proposals), but most authors have to court publishers, not the other way around.

I suppose someone from the outside could look at the websites that have published my work and feel that I have made it big—at least with respect to relationships with editors at popular evangelical websites. But every relationship with an editor did not come through my blog, although I suppose having the blog (and a local church pastorate) established a measure of legitimacy. My point is that, to my knowledge, no editors have ever looked at my blog saying, "Man, we need some posts from that guy."

Objective metrics help me because I fear the dangers of a sliding scale—the fear of thinking that to hit it big always means something more than where you currently are, something always just out of reach and around the corner,

---

[6] J. A. Medders, "Episode 14: Scott Sauls on Writing," *Home Row: A Podcast with Writers on Writing*, March 20, 2017, https://homerowpod.com/episodes/episode-14-scott-sauls-on-writing, and Chase Replogle, "Scott Sauls: The Dangers and Pitfalls of Platform," *PastorWriter*, June 18, 2018, https://pastorwriter.com/episode/21-scott-sauls-the-dangers-and-pitfalls-of-platform/.

something like rowing toward Gatsby's green light. An author hasn't hit it big until he's as well-known as, say, Timothy Keller. This is silly . . . and sinful. I'm a member of an online group for Christian writers, and we recently discussed blogging struggles. The most successful blogger among us commented, "One thing I can attest to is that if 'bigger' is your goal, nothing will ever be big enough . . . because 'bigger' isn't really a measure of having more readers than you do now, but having more readers than the other guy." This is the sliding scale I fear and the one that will bleed your joy and devour your contentment.

In that same online discussion group, I wrote that I had *not* hit it big in blogging. A friend asked what I meant by that. What I mean is that after blogging weekly for over six years, I have just over five hundred email subscribers. My open rate on emails is around 40%. That percentage floats just above industry standards for religious emails (per Mailchimp), which is good, but it also means only about two hundred people open each email I send. I suspect that far less than this go on to read the email they opened. My "click rate" within each email hovers around 1–2%, which is tiny. And almost no one except me ever shares my blog posts on social media. I only share each post at most once. By the way, allow me to break the fourth wall for a moment to interject that I'm not crying or upset and hopefully not ranting; I'm just disclosing what's behind the curtain.

At the end of last year a number of bloggers shared on social media their blog traffic from the previous year. A few friends of mine had tremendous years, which I loved and rejoiced over. My friend Chris, who asked me to define hitting it big, had web traffic numbers twice as big as my best year, which was twice as big as all my other years. That's objective, not subjective. I'm not complaining; I'm simply saying that over the last year, a year when I wrote more guest posts than ever and appeared on a few podcasts and published several longer projects, my blog subscribers stopped growing. Sure, I occasionally get new subscribers, but every email I send loses subscribers too, often several. All this happens while John and I write a book about blogging. A guy writing a book about blogging should be able to grow one.

If we could measure the number of people who read my posts—not measuring pageviews and those who only skimmed a paragraph or two but measuring those who actually read an entire post—I think the number of people reading my posts could be counted on two hands, or maybe two hands *and* two feet. I'd hardly say having seventeen people read each post qualifies as big readership. And over the last twelve months my blog might even be shrinking. Adding shorter paragraphs, more subheadings, lists, and hot takes would get more readers to skim my posts, yet I'll often find myself intentionally writing posts with long paragraphs and without headings, lists, and hot takes just to reward readers who read, like a parent putting a candy bar in the bottom of their kids' laundry baskets to reward them for staying the course until they finish the job.

The Battle for Facebook Shares and Internet Attention

Perhaps the shrinking of my readers has to do, in part, with my writing and blogging skills. Improving my ability to write subheadings and titles feels more legit than cultivating readers through spicy hot takes. So, I don't want to deflect ownership. I can write better than I do.

But my shrinking readership also reflects changes in culture and internet algorithms. With respect to culture, consider the migration of younger people from Facebook to Instagram, TikTok, and other social media platforms geared more toward pictures and videos than words. And the few words these platforms have do not tend to be reader friendly, having tiny character limits that allow only a taste of a full post (see also Instagram's common "link in bio" promise, which only delivers until supplanted by another link).

We've already hinted at the changes to algorithms in a few places in this book, but we need to mention it outright. Generating a large number of shares on Facebook does not happen today except by a few bloggers. Facebook algorithms want you to stay scrolling and liking and reading Facebook, not clicking away. It's the same with Google. It used to be that when you searched a question, you were given links to go browse. Of course Google still returns links, but more often than not, the top links are excerpts that show searchers the answers to their questions. So, if you crush the SEO on a post (which I rarely worry about) and Google ranks your post near the top or even at the top of all posts, you still might not get many click-overs because searchers only want the bite-sized answer, and Google feeds it to them.[7] For example, if you wrote an article about why analogies for the Trinity are unhelpful using those words in the title, and someone Googled, "Why are analogies for the Trinity unhelpful?" Google will likely return an excerpt of your post that gives away the best part. This is great for those using

---

[7] Michael Stelzner, "The Death of Google Search Traffic and What It Means for Marketers," *Social Media Examiner*, July 4, 2019, https://www.socialmediaexaminer.com/ death-google-search-traffic-what-it-means-for-marketers/.

Google but not so great for bloggers.[8] Tasty, free samples from Google don't always lead people to grab the meal.

Additionally, the idea that lead magnets generate hundreds of email subscribers has lost the novelty it once had. As much as I think serious bloggers should have something they give away in exchange for access to a person's inbox, what person really sits around thinking, "What I need is an inbox filled with more subscription emails"?

Not to mention that blogging also must compete with other platforms for attention. In Tony Reinke's book *Competing Spectacles*, he describes attention as a zero-sum commodity. "At some point we must close all our screens and fall asleep."[9] Reinke quotes the CEO of Microsoft who noted, "We are moving from a world where computing power was scarce to a place where it now is almost limitless, and where the true scarce commodity is increasingly human attention."[10] This certainly affects bloggers and blogging. Whatever you think of Michael Hyatt's famous book *Platform*, the subtitle makes a good point: getting noticed in a noisy world ain't easy. The streaming services of Netflix, Hulu, and Amazon Prime Video gobble up the precious resource of attention. Individual online authors and their blogs are left to compete for the table scraps of attention with large conglomerate blogs, Christian news ministries,

---

[8] There's nothing new under the sun. The push to simplify—really to oversimplify—began long ago. For example, in the middle of the nineteenth century Søren Kierkegaard said, "Not just in commerce but in the world of ideas too our age is putting on a veritable clearance sale. Everything can be had so dirt cheap that one begins to wonder whether in the end anyone will want to make a bid" (Søren Kierkegaard, *Fear and Trembling*, trans. Alastair Hannay [New York: Penguin Books, 2006], 3).

[9] Tony Reinke, *Competing Spectacles: Treasuring Christ in the Media Age* (Wheaton: Crossway, 2019), 57. Cf. Netflix CEO Reed Hastings who even said, "we actually compete with sleep" (Rina Raphael, "Netflix CEO Reed Hastings: Sleep Is Our Competition," *Fast Company*, November 6, 2017, https://www.fastcompany.com/40491939/netflix-ceo-reed-hastings-sleep-is-our-competition).

[10] Reinke, *Competing Spectacles*, 57

podcasts, YouTube channels, and the microblogging of Twitter threads and Instagram posts. A friend once told me that when it comes to playing outdoor sports (e.g., skiing, mountain biking, rock climbing, kayaking), you have to pick one or at most two because they're too expensive and time-consuming. The same could be said of excelling at a craft and cultivating an audience; it's a rare person who can excel across all the communication platforms available today to the dedicated amateur.

For all these reasons—the changing Facebook and Google algorithms, the cultural aversion to trading one's email address for subscriptions, and the crowded market of ideas vying for attention—the blogging landscape has changed, and so should our expectations for growth. Comparing the success of average bloggers today with the success of average bloggers just five and certainly ten years ago is like comparing baseball stats of today with the stats during the steroid era, which often get flagged with an asterisk.

The Battle in Our Hearts

We Christian bloggers have a strange relationship with metrics. We love them and hate them. We need pageviews to validate our labors, and we loathe the magnetism statistics have over us. It's not unlike the pastor who laments the Monday morning deluge of emails while at the same time knowing each inbox ping supplies a spurt of dopamine reassuring him of his job security and importance: *people need me—look how they email.* Deep down most Christian bloggers do want to write for the sake of God and his glory, for the sake of truth, for the sake of serving readers with our words. But I also know that for me, the mottos of "art for God's sake" and "art for ego's sake" slosh about in the same heart.

Professor and author John Koessler wrote on his blog, "What if, like Emily Dickinson, we die without seeing the bulk of what we have written published?"[11] It's a good question. Today bloggers can publish whatever we want as fast as we want, but most of us know what it means to self-publish posts long labored over only to hear crickets, which means there are more similarities to Dickinson and her mid-nineteenth century writing in obscurity than we might expect. Koessler continues, "The romantic in me says that it doesn't matter. I am a writer. Therefore, I must write. But it is often the pragmatist who sits at the keyboard. I am afraid I am wasting my time. I worry that no one is listening." While Koessler worries about no one listening, I often have the stats to prove no one was. So why keep blogging?

> Your metrics may only be telling you that fifty people read your post, but you will be surprised when that one lady from church, quiet and keeping to herself, mentions that she reads your posts often and draws encouragement from them. No analytic software captures that.
> – *Alex Kocman, alexkocman.com*

My reflections here about how I measure success as a blogger probably says more about me and my existential blogging angst than the actual topic, so please forgive me. But the point I'm trying to meander toward is seeing the goodness of what Laura Lundgren calls being a "village

---

[11] John Koessler, "Stop Shouting: A Few Quiet Thoughts About Writing & Publishing," *A Stranger in the House of God: John Koessler's Podcast and Weblog*, January 20, 2020, https://johnkoessler.com/2020/01/14/stop-shouting-a-few-quiet-thoughts-about-writing-publishing/.

poet."[12] A village poet views success as faithfully serving a small number of readers with our words, not as a resignation to the state of affairs but as a goal. The internet needs more Christian village poets. Tim Challies has pointed out that just because it feels like every major website in your blogging bubble has already written on a topic and thus saturated it, the reality is that many people in our local churches and who belong to our blog readership don't read the major ministry blog sites.[13] They need us to serve them. We have a vital role to play despite what the typical metrics of success tell us.

"When I first arrived," Lundgren writes, "the internet felt wide open with possibility." But she soon realized, as we all must realize of our own writing at some point, her writing wasn't as unique as she once believed. Other bloggers crowded her niche, and sometimes with content better than hers. However, rather than being crushed, she "began to see it as a reason to rejoice." Perhaps God placed her, she wonders, along with these other women bloggers all over his globe so that everyone could know a blogger with a hunger for Scripture and a passion for clear communication. Lundgren asks, "What if, instead of competing with other women writers or seeking a larger platform for my writing, I became the 'village poet' for my friends and neighbors and began to see other writers as my peers and friends?"

This is no small shift. In a world that expects and rewards all things done fast and famously, the biggest challenge for Christian writers might be to find joy in being faithful to God

[12] Laura Lundgren, "Village Poet," *Servants of Grace*, March 11, 2019, https://servantsofgrace.org/village-poet/.
[13] Tim Challies, "Why You Shouldn't Stop Blogging (or Why You Should Consider Starting)," *Challies.com*, January 10, 2019, https://www.challies.com/articles/why-you-shouldnt-stop-blogging-or-why-you-should-consider-starting/.

through our faithfulness with the little things. Lundgren goes on to say, "My writing has not turned into a career. It's mostly a hobby and a privilege. As a village poet I recognize that my writing is only one aspect of a larger ministry. Writing gives me a chance to order my thoughts about Scripture, but the ultimate goal is not to write well about these things but to live them out in obedience and humility."

I think Lundgren gets what it means to hit it big blogging in a clickbait world: Art displayed on the fridge for Abba and for a few of his people. We wrote this book to help your heart get it too.

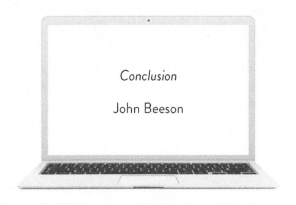

Conclusion

John Beeson

LIFTING HIM HIGH

How Do I Cultivate a Cross-Shaped Blog?

W ould you say God's ambitions are modest? I think not. The book of Revelation gives us a glimpse at the ambitions God has for his world. He is going to destroy sin and death and create the new heavens and new earth. Fairly ambitious, right?

In his book *Rescuing Ambition* Dave Harvey argues that ambition has got a bad rap. "True humility doesn't kill our dreams; it provides a guardrail for them," he says.[1] The problem with our aspirations isn't that they are too big. Problems arise when our aspirations don't align with God's. Don't shy away from our magnetic pull toward glory. Instead, make certain that it pulls us toward the King of glory. As Paul Tripp says, "You were hardwired by your Creator for a glory orientation. It is inescapable. It's in your genes."[2]

---

[1] Dave Harvey, *Rescuing Ambition* (Wheaton: Crossway, 2020), 14.
[2] Paul Tripp, *A Quest for More: Living for Something Bigger Than You* (Greensboro, NC: New Growth Press, 2007), 18.

That's pretty freeing, don't you think? That longing for grandeur and for a lasting legacy was given to you by your Creator. The issue isn't the glory orientation; the issue is its alignment. Our heart whispers lies about what will satisfy our longing for glory. We think praise and a platform will satisfy. But no amount of readers will ever satisfy, and no pat on the back from your favorite author will make you content.

My platform will never fix my insecurities. Praises will never grant me security. No book deal will ever fill that hole in my heart.

Where can our glory orientation be satisfied? Jesus's life had an outrageous glory orientation. And yet, where is that glory orientation ultimately fulfilled? At the cross. The apostle John refers to the lifting up of Christ on the cross as his great moment of glory. Christ being physically lifted up on the cross was ultimately his moment of being lifted up in glory. In John 12, John records this interaction between Jesus, his Father, and a crowd,

> "Now is my soul troubled. And what shall I say? 'Father, save me from this hour'? But for this purpose I have come to this hour. Father, glorify your name." Then a voice came from heaven: "I have glorified it, and I will glorify it again." The crowd that stood there and heard it said that it had thundered. Others said, "An angel has spoken to him." Jesus answered, "This voice has come for your sake, not mine. Now is the judgment of this world; now will the ruler of this world be cast out. And I, when I am lifted up from the earth, will draw all people to myself." He said this to show by what kind of death he was going to die. (John 12:27–33)

How is the Father going to glorify his name? Through the crucifixion of Jesus. We embrace our glory orientation most perfectly when our lives are most cross-shaped.

In their book *Influence,* Kate Motaung and Shannon Popkin liken a platform to a lifeguard stand built not to elevate the lifeguard but for the sake of the swimmers. They reflect, "A platform should be the structure from which we serve others, not ourselves. When you and I step onto our God-given platforms, our goal should be to elevate Jesus, not ourselves. Our message should lead others to His story and glory, not our own."[3]

God has given you gifts and relationships and lifeguard stands, and he has called you to use them for his glory. No one else writes like you write. No one else has the same sphere of influence that you have. You know the names and faces of readers whom we'll never know—but God knows them and loves them. From the perch of your lifeguard platform, focus on what God has given you, not on what he hasn't given you. Don't obsess over what your blog can become or where it can get you; rather, let your focus be serving your readers and glorifying God. Lift others up, and lift Christ up higher still.

In the introduction we shared that blogging for God's glory means,

first, to have our motivations aligned with God's, and

second, to pursue excellence in the craft, including theological precision, beautiful prose, visual appeal, and the

[3] Motaung and Popkin, *Influence*, 6.

edification of readers, all drawing from the best industry practices.

We hope this book has challenged you to align your motivations a bit more closely with God's and has given you a clearer understanding of how God might be calling you to pursue excellence in your craft. We genuinely desire to serve you. If you want to reach out, we would be honored to see how we can serve you. Our emails are <u>john@thebeehive.live</u> and <u>benjamin@fanandflame.com</u>.

May we, as a community of fellow bloggers, make much of Christ together.

APPENDICES

IS BLOGGING DEAD?

Twenty-Six Bloggers Weigh In

I n a series of quick, mindless thumb swipes to the top of my Twitter feed, my eyes notice a tweet of someone John and I respect—someone who thinks deeply about blogging and journalism and reaching people for Christ via the internet.

His tweet declares that blogs have been killed.

I take a deep breath and sit zombie-like on my couch.

I stare out the window for a bit, contemplating why a book about blogging wouldn't also die as collateral damage. *Who needs a book about blogging if blogging is dead?* Though we've already written the first draft of this book, it sure would save us a lot of time and money to cut our losses.

Collin Hansen is the editorial director of The Gospel Coalition, and for several years he co-led the now-disbanded group called "Band of Bloggers." In other words, he knows more than a little about the topic of blogging.

Hansen's tweet identified what, in his opinion, killed blogging: "Social media killed blogs," he writes. "Can't find them any longer, since folks don't browse sites any longer."[1] His comment sat in a thread discussing the current fad of writers using e-newsletters rather than true blogs, a topic that obviously interests John and me.

As much as I respect Hansen, I'd suggest we not order the autopsy report yet. To tweak the words often ascribed to Mark Twain, the reports of the death of blogs have been greatly exaggerated. I agree that today's blogger cannot ascend to the levels of influence reached almost exclusively by those who got into the game ten years ago, if not twenty. But I think we'd be wrong to say social media has killed blogs, just as we'd be wrong to say the car killed the bicycle. For exercise and for pleasure and for social interaction, people still ride—just as people will blog. Think how many Twitter handles still have a link to the person's blog? Lots, I tell you, lots. Admittedly, when I click those links I'm often disappointed by the result: the last post dates from more than a year ago and the post before that is often even further back—hence why we wrote this book. Tim Challies highlights a potential incentive to commit or recommit to blogging as others bail. "With so many people opting out," he writes, "there is lots of room for aspiring writers to work their way in."[2]

Samuel James is more pessimistic. He writes,

Blogging is dead, right? At least among the folks in a

[1] Collin Hansen (@collinhansen), Twitter post, September 2, 2019, 4:36 p.m. "Social media killed blogs. Can't find them any longer, since folks don't browse sites any longer," https://twitter.com/collinhansen/status/1169711035042934784.

[2] Tim Challies, "Why Christians Blogs Aren't What They Used to Be," *Challies.com*, April 25, 2018, https://www.challies.com/articles/when-christian-blogs-began-to-change/.

position to say so, this seems to be the consensus. Many of blogging's most important early practitioners have either abandoned it . . . or else transformed their writing spaces into storefronts that offer "promoted" content in exchange for patronage. The thinking goes like this: Before Mark Zuckerberg and Tweet threads, blogging was a viable way of sharing ideas online. Now, though, social media has streamlined and mobilized both content and community. Reading a blog when you could be reading what your friends are Tweeting about is like attending a lecture completely alone. It's boring and lonely for you, and a waste of time for the lecturer.[3]

The full post by James suggests more optimism than that quote belies. For example, after noting many strengths of blogging in our cultural moment, his concluding paragraph states, "Blogging still matters, because it's still the medium that most ably combines the best aspects of online writing."[4]

Twitter doesn't do nuance well, so as I think back over Collin Hansen's statement about the death of blogging, perhaps he only meant that blogs don't have the popularity they used to have or that many obstacles are stacked against their success, as James points out and all of us would likely concede.

Regardless, I am still blogging regularly. So is John. And so are hundreds of thousands of others. If you're reading this book, we want you to keep blogging or consider starting a blog of your own if you don't have one yet. Bloggers writing for the glory of God have not saturated the market, not even

---

[3] Samuel James, "Why Blogging Still Matters: Why Dedicated Online Writing Spaces Might Be the Cure for Our Social Media Ills," *Letters and Liturgy*, March 22, 2018, https://letterandliturgy.com/2018/03/22/why-blogging-still-matters/.

[4] Ibid.

close. Author Tony Reinke spoke about this in an interview on the *Home Row* podcast.

> Don't be intimidated by all the books. Everybody is publishing it seems. [But] we have this promise from the Lord in Habakkuk. It says, "The earth will be filled with the knowledge of the glory of the Lord as the waters cover the sea" (2:14). Just think about that. Think about that overwhelming tsunami of the knowledge of God. We are far from that saturation point.... There is so much work to be done.[5]

I agree with Reinke. We have work to do, books and blog posts to write, and the glory of God to spread. If you ask John and me, the fridge is big enough for more blog posts.

But don't just take our word for it. We asked a few dozen other bloggers to give us their hot take on the future of blogging, because offering hot takes is all we bloggers do. Right?

Is Blogging Dead?

> It seems unlikely that blogging will ever be as popular as it was in the late 1990s, but people continue to want to read blog-like content. The form it takes may be different (people, for example, seem to want to turn platforms that were not designed for blogging, such as Instagram, into blogs), but the blog-like intention behind the content persists.
>
> Abby Farson Pratt, <u>abbyfp.com</u>

Although it's easy to think that blogging has already had its heyday, the demand for long-form content, while tempered

---

[5] J. A. Medders, "Interview with Tony Reinke," *Home Row: A Podcast with Writers on Writing*, April 11, 2016, https://jamedders.com/home-row-tony-reinke-writing/.

by market forces, will always be a factor. Search engines like Google assign more weight to long-form content. While those less serious about writing turn to social media to express themselves, more opportunity now exists in the blogging arena for those committed to persevering in their craft and doing the hard work of building an audience over time.

Alex Kocman, *alexkocman.com*

Bloggers are in a unique position to inform people that they wouldn't be able to reach otherwise, and they have the benefit of being able to speak on any topic. If blogs are being used correctly, to build people up in their faith and inform believers for God's glory, then I believe they will always have a place.

Alistair Chalmers, *achalmersblog.com*

In my opinion, blogging is not dead. Although the word "blogging" might sound outdated, just call it an "article," or a "writing," or even an "essay," and voila! You're back to blogging.

Alisa Childers, *alisachilders.com*

I think that blogging has shifted. Where we used to sign up to follow blogs, we now follow accounts—Instagram, Twitter, Facebook. With the inundation of information, I wonder if we've become lazy—wanting our social media to vet our posts for us and to make it easier and quicker to decide what we will spend time reading. I don't think blogging has disappeared. There are new blogs every day. I think the way that people view and interact with blogs has shifted. I think it affects the reader and the writer at the same time, and it's a phenomenon that new writers and blog owners will have to deal with. In order to get followings, you will feel the push to promote, promote, promote. That being said, I do wonder as Facebook, Twitter, and others all come under fire for their filtering, if more and more people will start to take control over what content they want to see. To be honest, and perhaps this is more cynical, but I see the majority of people complaining but then continuing on with what is easiest.

Brianna Lambert, *lookingtotheharvest.com*

Not at all! Social media has its place, and I know microblogging is on the rise on those platforms, but I think they serve different purposes. First, there's the issue of space—you simply cannot flesh out a nuanced idea in the narrow confines of social media in the same way as a longer blog post. Second, your reach on social media has become so dependent upon algorithms. We see what the platforms want us to see, and we don't have control over that. Blogging allows us to curate our own sources and see every post by visiting specific sites or using an RSS reader. Blogging occupies a crucial space between social media and books, and we'd be poorer without it.

Cassie Watson, *casswatson.com*

I think a website is still essential, and including a blog is a helpful way of demonstrating commitment and credibility. But a blog no longer seems to be enough. Podcasts and YouTube are becoming more important platforms because they possess greater attention.

Chase Replogle, *chasereplogle.com*

Blogging is still an incredibly important means of communication, especially in the Christian space. Its day is not over, even if it looks a bit different.

Chris Martin, *chrismartin.blog*

Blogging has a future, though like many mediums in this age, it may need to find new iterations. Even in the short time blogging has already experienced, we've seen a transformation of style and presentation—some that have been helpful and others less so.

Chris Thomas, *ploughmansrest.com*

Blogging is dead in terms of the early blogs that primarily curate info available elsewhere on the internet. Blogs that did that well are still alive and well but they own the market. Those who own that lane do enough research and reflection to also give a lot of insights into any number of topics. Blogging isn't dead in terms of writers who are able to give thoughtful insights and perspectives on important issues. The newer brand of blogging isn't for people who merely want to air their opinions but for those who possess the time, skill, and energy to produce something unique and helpful. There's always a space for committed authors who want to help others. But like most things, it takes hard work and anyone wanting a fastlane to "success" will likely drop out long before they get enough traction to make a lasting contribution.

Dan DeWitt, *theolatte.com*

Yes and no. Yes in the sense that the newness and buzz of blogging probably will never be what it once was. I also say no because I don't think blogging will die anytime soon. As others have pointed out, the name "blogging" might change. But the format of writing words in article form to post on the internet to promote edification isn't going away soon, so I think blogging has a bright future.

David Qaoud, *gospelrelevance.com*

Blogging as a thing "everybody does" is gone, but that's not necessarily a bad thing. Writers who want to test a message, have unedited freedom in voice and style, hone their craft, and develop a body of work will keep plodding. Although not always the most efficient way of getting a piece to the masses, those who stick around will hopefully make blogging about the value of truthful words and vibrant stories.

Emily Jensen & Laura Wifler, *risenmotherhood.com*

Our world increasingly seems to value forms of communication that are instantaneous, combative, and designed to trigger emotions. Against this trend, many are recognizing just how important long-form mediums are for creating light, not just heat. Blogging is a kind of hybrid medium— faster than books, longer than Twitter. My hope is that Christians will continue to engage the world of blogging as we try to carve out spaces for reflection and reasoned dialogue.

Gavin Ortlund, *gavinortlund.com*

I work with young writers every week, and I firmly believe blogging is not dead. How blogs are curated and shared has shifted and evolved over the years, but blogs' power and purpose have not. Blogging is still a medium that changes lives and contributes to the kingdom, one post at a time.

Jaquelle Ferris, *jaquellecrowe.com*

I'm late to the game and can't say for sure. It does seem like things like YouTube are taking over. But, I still read others' blogs, and other people still read mine, so I think there's still a small space for it in the world and in ministry.

Jen Oshman, *jenoshman.com*

The original kind of blogging is done and gone. Few remain. More collective groups are writing better content with editors, and that is far superior in my opinion.

Jeremy Writebol, *jwritebol.net*

Yes and no. Blogging has certainly peaked because, as many people discovered, it's easy to start a blog but hard to maintain interest in writing for one on a regular basis. But blogging is still essential because the low barrier to entry allows undiscovered talent to flourish.

Joe Carter, *thegospelcoalition.org/profile/joe-carter*

Blogging is *definitely* dead!!! (Actually, it is a pet peeve of mine to see the headline formula, "Is _____ dead?" The subject in question never actually dies; it just changes. Unless you're talking about VHS or Laserdisc players, then they're dead alright.) Blogging isn't dead, but it has changed due to podcasts, YouTube, and Twitter. A certain type of blogging has had its day. But there is still room for thoughtful and well-written blogging.

Kevin Halloran, *kevinhalloran.net*

I don't believe so. These days, Twitter and Facebook have reduced our attention spans to only be capable of digesting small, bite-sized pieces of information before moving on to the next thing, many times without critically reflecting upon the tweet or post we've just read. Blogging provides a great platform for more rigorously interacting with and explaining ideas in a way that is still open to community and peer feedback without as much distraction. I hope that our society, as time goes on, will become disenchanted with shallow information grazing, and come to appreciate this medium more and more. This will be more likely if the blogosphere is already filled with quality, Christ-centered content once the rest of the world comes back here.

Kris Sinclair, *krissinclair.com*

Nah. Especially since social media is stupid and people are becoming more suspicious of its integrity. I think more people will transition from social media to blogs and email communication.

Kristen Wetherell, *kristenwetherell.com*

I think the world of blogging has certainly changed. But, I don't think that the medium is going anywhere. I do think that it looks different, and maybe the day of the mega-blog is passing us by. Bloggers are going to have to be satisfied with smaller audiences, with more of a niche following, because there is so much out there that distinguishing yourself as a big blog that everyone checks constantly is getting more and more impossible. This is especially true of Christian blogs because, let's face it, the Christian message is getting less and less appealing as our culture steps further away from Jesus. I write things that people tell me they agree with but are afraid to share because of the inevitable backlash from their friends and family. In that way, Christian bloggers are certainly operating in the land of Jesus's words about what the gospel does: "Do not think that I have come to bring peace to the earth. I have not come to bring peace, but a sword. For I have come to set a man against his father, and a daughter against her mother, and a daughter-in-law against her mother-in-law. And a person's enemies will be those of his own household" (Matt 10:34–36).

Melissa Edgington, *yourmomhasablog.com*

Blogging is not done yet. It has a few and new competitors along the way. As long as the passion is there, we don't have to throw in the towel yet. We just need to find new and exciting ways to be heard.

Nitoy Gonzales, *delightinggrace.wordpress.com*

No, because it will continue to play a role in supporting the mission of the local church. It may begin to look different, e.g., smaller circles of influence, more local writing, etc. But if we see the role of blogging as falling in line with furthering the mission of the church and building up the saints for the work of ministry, then it will continue to have purpose because it falls in line with God's mission.

Ryan Williams, *amicalled.com*

Blogging isn't going to go away, but the influence and reach of individual bloggers will probably never be what it was ten years ago. There's so much content out there right now, and ways to curate that content through algorithms, that only people with specific kinds of day jobs can afford to "build" a blogging profile.

Samuel James, *letterandliturgy.com*

Blogging is not dead because Jesus is not dead. Christians have always looked for ways to share the gospel and to share what they are learning about how the gospel shapes our lives. As long as we have the internet and the opportunity to post on the internet, Christian bloggers will write about this best of news. It is why I have blogged for over nine years, and why I plan to be blogging nine years from now.

Tim Counts, _hemustbecomegreater.com_

No. It's just transformed for some into the microblogging of Twitter and Facebook. It's still a kind of blog, just smaller and easier to digest. Long-form blogging isn't dead. When TV was invented, people thought movie theaters would die out. They didn't.

Tom Terry, _tomthinking.com_

No. It's true that the season of early blogging, in which upstart bloggers could build a platform by quality writing on a large variety of subjects, has come to an end. For a new blog to gain traction today, one needs either an already-established platform or excellent insights that focus on a narrower sliver of topics. But blogging itself—which is really just one form of writing articles, similar to newspaper columns from a hundred years ago from good writers—is still and will remain a relevant form of communication. Social media has grown in importance for blogging, as most readers interact with writers by following social media accounts and not blogs. But this doesn't mean that blogging has died, only that the entry point to these articles has shifted.

Trevin Wax, _thegospelcoalition.org/blogs/trevin-wax_

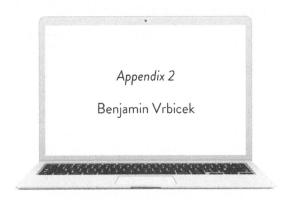

Appendix 2

Benjamin Vrbicek

GLOSSARY

Eighty-Eight Words and Phrases Bloggers Should Learn

404 Page   webpage a visitor is redirected to after clicking a broken link to an otherwise functioning website. To check a website's 404 page, add "/404.php" after the domain name (e.g., benjaminvrbicek.com/404.php).

Above the fold   visible portion of a website before you scroll down. It was originally a newspaper term that describes the part of the newspaper readers can see without unfolding the paper.

Affiliate marketing   promotion of a product that leads to a small commission for the website owner when a customer buys a product. Participants must typically be approved for enrollment in an affiliate program. The most popular affiliate partnership for bloggers is with Amazon.

Algorithm   complex formula used to make a decision. The specifics of an algorithm are often veiled to outsiders, for example, when Facebook algorithms determine which posts appear in your timeline.

Alt-text (alternate text)   words inserted in metadata to describe a picture on the internet. The description is not typically seen by a reader. Alt-text is read by web crawlers and is also intended to help the blind and visually impaired using screen readers to understand what is on an internet page.

Analytics   detailed statistics about a website's traffic; for example, how many emails are opened, how many times pages are viewed, and how readers are accessing your website.

Automated email   email reply automatically sent when a person subscribes to an email list, often welcoming the person to the list and extending the promised lead magnet, such as an ebook.

Avatar   icon or image that represents a user in an internet forum or video game, or simply the profile picture used by your account.

Blog   in the late 90s the phrase "web log" described posts where users cataloged their thoughts. These two words were combined and shortened to create the word blog.

Blog farm   website built from a group of linked blogs. The largest in the Christian world is probably Patheos.

Blog roll   list of blogs endorsed by a particular blogger. In the early days of blogging, blog rolls helped readers find other like-minded blogs. The advent of social media and other internet changes have made blog rolls obsolete.

Blogosphere   all blogging websites on the internet, collectively.

Bounce rate   measure of how quickly a visitor leaves a website after first arriving. A high bounce rate means users left quickly, and a low bounce rate means readers stayed longer and browsed more content.

Broken link   links that no longer direct users to active webpages and instead return an error message. If the broken link is an internal link on your website, it will take visitors to your 404 page. If the broken link is an external link, it will take visitors to that website's 404 page, unless the whole website is defunct, in which case the user will receive some other error message.

Call to action (CTA)   response that a web designer desires a visitor to take upon arriving at a website. Common examples include "sign up," "schedule a phone call," "find out more," and "buy the book."

CAPTCHA   checkbox or other test at the end of a form to confirm that the reader is human, not a robot. CAPTCHA is an acronym for Completely Automated Public Turing test to tell Computers and Humans Apart.

Category   grouping of similar content under one name or phrase. Blog posts are typically marked in one or more categories to help readers find similar posts, for example, the category of "Book Reviews," "Preaching," or "Blogging." Categories are broader than *tags*, which tend to be very specific.

Clickbait   pejorative term for content, especially titles and images, designed to get visitors to click. The term is loosely drawn from fishing where shiny bait attracts the attention of a fish but conceals the hook. To some degree, what constitutes clickbait is in the eye of the beholder; however, standard tropes are readily identifiable.

Comments   feature on a blog that allows for readers to respond to posts, typically underneath the post. Comments can be enabled or disabled.

Collaborative blog   blog where multiple bloggers post on a single site. Also called a group blog.

Content management system (CMS)   another name for a platform that does a certain function. So, for example, blogging content management systems include WordPress and Squarespace, and email content management systems include Constant Contact and ConvertKit.

Conversions   when a reader takes the desired action of the web designer, for example, signing up for an email list or webinar or buying your book or course. Conversions are typically described as a percentage of the number of pageviews, so a certain landing page might be described as converting 5% of readers.

Cookie   data that a website stores on a user's computer while the user is browsing the site. Website logins, for example, use cookies to remember usernames and passwords (also called internet cookie, web cookie, and browser cookie).

Crawler   "tentacles" of a search engine that explore websites and report back to the search engine with information about the site. The process of searching websites and cataloging their content is called indexing.

Creative Commons   non-profit organization that curates creative work such as photography that the public is free to use.

Dashboard   behind-the-scenes area of a blog to add posts, change themes or templates, view analytics, and make other changes to the website.

Drip campaign   series of automated emails that someone receives upon signing up to an email list. Drip campaigns may teach a course, help a subscriber become familiar with an organization, or encourage subscribers toward the purchase of a product.

Domain   primary internet address of a website. The domain includes both the letters before the extension and the extension
itself (.com, .net, .org, etc.). A domain name that is preceded by
"http://", "https://", or "www." and followed by a slash ("/")
and then more letters is called a website address or URL. For
example, *Mailchimp.com* is a domain name, while *https://mail-
chimp.com/pricing/* is an address. To make it easier for readers
to identify the words in a domain name, they are often written
with intercase text, meaning both uppercase and lowercase letters (e.g., desiringGod). The domain name brings readers to the
homepage of a website, while an address takes you to a specific
page.

Double opt-in   when a subscriber joins a list by filling out a
form, the subscriber has then opted-in. A double opt-in requires subscribers to then open and click a confirmation email
before they are officially added to the list. Double opt-in helps
prevent bad email addresses from getting on a list. Having to
look for and click a link in the confirmation email also encourages subscribers to search their spam or junk email folders,
which is where some subscription emails get placed.

Draft   post that is in process and not yet published (i.e., made
public) on a website.

Email list   list of email addresses that have subscribed to receive
updates from a website. The email list may or may not also con-
tain additional information such as name and address. When
using an email content management system, many other details will be collected and added to the list, including IP
address, opt-in time, and data about open rates.

Engagement   amount of shares, comments, emails, and other interaction a website or blog post generates.

Evergreen   website content that does not go out of season. In the
context of Christian blogging, this often includes devotional

posts and reflections on Scripture or perennial themes that are not too closely tied to a cultural moment or season.

Favicon   small logo for a website at the top of a browser window that also becomes visible when a user bookmarks a website. The branding of a favicon should have symmetry with the branding of the associated website.

Footer   bottom of a website that remains the same across every page of the site, typically having things such as contact information, social media links, a subscribe feature, and navigation links similar to but also simpler than what appears in the menu on a website's header.

Funnel   specific type of website designed to lead visitors toward a desired action such as the purchasing of a product. Funnels are also known as sales or marketing funnels. For practical purposes, it might be said that a sales funnel functions like a strong, focused, and often singular call to action.

Google Ads (formerly Google Adwords)   marketing program that allows a website owner to pay to have a webpage listed at the top of a Google web search. When purchasing these ads, users pick a list of keywords related to the content they wish to promote. Users set a monthly budget for their ads but only pay when their promoted links are clicked.

Google Adsense   program to run ads on your website through Google. For these ads to be profitable, the website needs a high level of traffic. Google places ads tailored to your website niche and the personal browsing information of visitors. Google pays a website owner when users click the ads.

Google Analytics   robust way to track statistics about a website. Google Analytics must be installed.

Guest post   when someone other than the main author writes a post for a blog.

Header   part of the website visible at the top of the page, often having a logo, search bar, and a navigational menu.

Host   where the information from a website is stored. Depending on the website platform—which is also known as a content management system or CMS—the website may be *hosted* or *self-hosted*. The storage for a hosted website is provided by the website platform, whereas with a self-hosted website, the storage is done through another company.

HTML   stands for Hypertext Markup Language, the coding language utilized by web designers to build a website's look and functionality. Websites built from a template often require little to no use of HTML by the user.

Hyperlink   link to a webpage, often highlighted by an underline and a color different from the surrounding text.

Infographic   visual display of information, often of statistics displayed artfully.

IP address   unique number separated by periods that identifies information about an internet user's location in the world (e.g., 166.89.49.126). IP stands for Internet Protocol.

Keyword   words and phrases commonly searched for in search engines. Keywords can either be short-tail, meaning they are more broad (e.g., theology) or they can be long-tail, meaning more specific (e.g., reformed theology R. C. Sproul).

Kicker   either the introduction to a journalistic article or the closing sentence or paragraph that summarizes the piece. When a kicker refers to the beginning of a piece, it is often set in a different font to draw attention. When a kicker refers to the end of an article, it often has in mind a summary of the piece but also an artful and even punchy statement that causes readers to think about an implication of the article.

Lead magnet   what marketers offer potential subscribers in exchange for their contact information and signing up to an email list. Typical lead magnets include ebooks, instructional courses, checklists, and swipe files.

Lede   opening sentence or paraphrase of a news story summarizing the most important details of the story. To *bury the lede* is to hide the most important information of an article, whether intentionally or unintentionally.

Link-back   link from one website to another, often present in the bio section of an author when guest posting on another website. Also called a *backlink*.

Listicle   shortened word form of the phrase *list-article*. A listicle structures the article in the form of a list, typically with short paragraphs under each item.

Metadata   identifying information about a website, webpage, or specific content on a webpage like a picture. Metadata includes information such as author, date, and keywords, which may or may not be visible to readers but is visible to search engine crawlers.

Menu bar   tool to navigate through specific webpages such as the homepage, about page, etc. Menu bars typically appear at the top of a website and may have drop-down options to navigate to more specific pages.

Nut graph   tight summary of the main point of an article. In journalism, the nut graph typically appears in the first few sentences.

Open-source   product that has been created and released to the public for use free of charge. Often it refers to code that can be built upon and manipulated.

Pageviews number of times a webpage receives a visitor. Pageviews are often casually conflated with the number of times a page has been read, but this cannot be measured; only the number of pageviews and perhaps how long users remained on the webpage can be counted.

Pay-per-click (PPC) method of advertising that pays advertisers for each click of a link and charges those who purchased the ad space. Readers who click the link are neither paid nor charged.

Permalink unique URL of a blog post designed to ensure that ongoing traffic is sent to the post.

Ping notification sent to a website owner that somewhere on the internet a link was published that points back to said website.

Platform the size of a person's influence, often measured through social media followers and email list subscribers.

Plugin code installed on a website to perform specific functions. The code for plugins can be free or paid.

Pop-up marketing tool that shows a window to visitors, often calling them to an action like subscribe or buy. The window can be programmed to appear only under certain scenarios, such as when a visitor first arrives, scrolls to a certain location on the page (e.g., the middle or bottom), or after a certain length of time on the website (e.g., ten or thirty seconds).

Monetize implementing ways of generating income through a website through such things as advertising or selling a product.

Return on investment (ROI) measure of the benefit accrued compared to investment. Return on investment can be stated as a future projection on returns or as actual returns.

Round-up post   collection of articles often around a theme and containing either a short introduction to the article or a quote from it. In the world of evangelical blogging, Tim Challies's daily *A La Carte* emails are the most popular round-up posts.

RSS   stands for Real Simple Syndication. An *RSS feed* allows users to subscribe to internet content (typically blogs, vlogs, and podcasts) from specific websites and have the website's content curated and delivered. An *RSS Aggregator* is software used to read *RSS feeds*.

Search Engine Optimization (SEO)   tailoring your website content to receive traffic from searches.

Sidebar   vertical area along the side of a website that displays navigational information including blog categories, tags, authors, and dates of posts grouped by certain intervals like months or years.

Single opt-in   when a subscriber joins a list by filling out a form, the subscriber has then opted-in. A single opt-in requires nothing more from users than filling out the form. Single opt-in streamlines the process of subscribing, which helps increase the number of subscribers, but it does also increase the chances that an email was mistyped or not sent to an active address.

Slug   a few words that describe a post or a page, which are usually a version of the post title. Generally it is the portion of the permalink (URL) that follows ".com/".

Spam   email or other form of unsolicited communication. Bloggers who sign up readers to their blog without consent are spamming those readers.

Sponsorship   intentional promotion of a product or person based on an existing relationship, often a formal relationship where money is involved.

Subscriber   someone who belongs to an email list of a blog, meaning the person receives updates to the blog as often as the website owner chooses to send them. The number of subscribers is one of several key metrics for assessing the size of the influence of a blog. For an individual Christian blogger (i.e., not a company website or a ministry website like The Gospel Coalition), many would consider fifty subscribers small; five hundred medium; five thousand large; and fifty thousand huge.

Swipe file   collection of downloadable information that others can use, often containing proven sales copy from previous promotions.

Tag   marker that identifies a theme in a particular post, often more specific than a blog post's category.

Tag cloud   visual representation of all of the tags used on a blog. Sometimes the words used more frequently are larger.

Template   pre-built website or email format that designers populate with content specific to the website. Templates can be free or paid and vary in their ability to be customized.

Theme   similar to a template, a pre-built website or email format with a certain visual look.

Traffic   number of visitors a website receives within a given time period.

Tripwire   product offered to subscribers shortly after opting in to a list, typically offered only for a short time and at a discount.

Troll   internet provocateurs who inflame conflict and grind an ax. Trolls tend to congregate under large "bridges" and comment sections and have blank avatars.

URL   internet web address for a single webpage. The acronym stands for Uniform Resource Locator.

Viral   content that gets extremely popular in a short time period.

Vlog   website, or portion thereof, that primarily posts video content the way bloggers primarily post words.

Widget   add-on to a WordPress website that performs a specific function such as adding social media icons or tweaking the form and function of a sidebar.

WordPress.com   free, simpler version of WordPress.

WordPress.org   paid, complex version of WordPress.

ABOUT THE AUTHORS

BENJAMIN VRBICEK and his wife Brooke have six children. Benjamin enjoys reading, wrestling with his children, dating his wife, eating at Chipotle, and riding his bicycle in the early hours of the morning. He earned a degree in mechanical and aerospace engineering from the University of Missouri and a masters of divinity from Covenant Theological Seminary in St. Louis, Missouri. He is a teaching pastor at Community Evangelical Free Church in Harrisburg, Pennsylvania. He is coauthor of *More People to Love* and *Enduring Grace*, and author of *Don't Just Send a Resume* and *Struggle Against Porn*. He blogs regularly at Fan and Flame and has also written for The Gospel Coalition, Desiring God, For The Church, 9Marks, Gospel-Centered Discipleship, and Christianity Today.

JOHN BEESON and his wife Angel have two children. John enjoys reading, Thai and Sonoran Mexican food, and watching or playing just about any sport. He received his undergraduate degree at Gordon College and his masters of divinity from Princeton Theological Seminary in Princeton, New Jersey. He is a co-lead pastor at New Life Bible Fellowship in Tucson, Arizona. He blogs at thebeehive.live and has written for The Gospel Coalition, For The Church, and Preach It Teach It. This is John's first book, and he is looking forward to his second, coming out in 2021, a book co-written with his wife called *Substitute Identities*.

ACKNOWLEDGMENTS

From Benjamin: This book started with John before either of us knew it would be a book. Five years ago I wrote down a series of questions for John to ponder as he launched his blog. Actually, I didn't write them. I used my phone's voice-to-text feature to record my stream-of-consciousness thoughts while my children played in a McDonald's Play-Place. I cleaned the questions up a bit, sent them to John, and we talked on the phone for ninety minutes. A year later, I polished those questions brighter and wrote them into a blog post. I hoped the questions would help others launch blogs that would glorify God. I feared, however, only five people would read the post. After I submitted the article to two different online publications and received rejections from each, I suspected editors also thought only five people would read the posts. But then I submitted it to *For The Church*, who published the article in the spring of 2018. Tim Challies shared a link to that post on his blog, and from there, Bill Feltner, the host of the show *His People* on Pilgrim Radio, saw the link and asked me for an interview to discuss Christian blogging. The interview made me wonder if there could be more to this topic than a few blog posts and an interview could cover. Eventually I circled back to John with the idea for this book. John, thank you for running this race with me; when we began the project I never expected the book would become such an expansive resource for bloggers. Thank you for being a friend, encourager, and someone to swap stories with of blogging highs and lows. I could not have written this book without you, and I wouldn't have wanted to.

Alexandra Richter has poured over each word in each book I've written, and most of my published articles. Alexandra, I confess, I never know when to write *who* or *whom*, so I avoid writing sentences that feel ambiguous. But I know that if I did write a sentence that needed a *who* or perhaps a *whom*, you'd know when I needed which. And thank you for caring as much, if not more, about the theology as the grammar. Speaking of grammar, thank you Russ Meek and Cassie Watson for also helping us catch the little mistakes that make a big difference.

I've never had an acknowledgment section in my books; I think I feared the cliché of it all. Expected or not, thank you, Brooke. There would be no books or blogs without your blessing.

From John: I couldn't imagine a better experience writing a book. It truly took a tribe to write this book and the leader of that tribe is you, Benjamin. Thanks for envisioning this book and for asking me to come along for the ride. The journey alone was worth it. You're a good friend and it's been a joy to follow your lead.

The biggest surprise for me in this process were the many cheerleaders who gathered around us and contributed in small and big ways. The writers' community at Gospel-Centered Discipleship was a constant source of encouragement. Thanks to each of you.

Thank you, New Life Bible Fellowship, for allowing me to write as your pastor as part of my ministry. I don't take that for granted. Thank you to the subscribers of The Bee Hive for every post you read, every comment you make, and every friend you share the blog with. I'm grateful for you.

My biggest cheerleaders are in my home. I love you, Angel, Camille, and Soren. Thank you for helping me steward this calling and for being my first and most important congregation.

From Us: Thank you, Tim Challies, for writing the foreword. Your generosity of giving away clicks to lesser-known writers extends far beyond your daily email. Thank you for being the kind of godfather of evangelical blogging that continues to care about your blogging godchildren.

Thank you to the community of Christian bloggers who helped make this book better. We especially want to thank those readers who poured over the manuscript the summer before we published. You filled a Google Doc with nearly a thousand edits to improve the prose.

Abigail Rehmert	abigailrehmert.com
Alistair Chalmers	achalmersblog.com
Bob Allen	inpursuit.blog
Brianna Lambert	lookingtotheharvest.com
Cassie Watson	casswatson.com
Chris Thomas	ploughmansrest.com
David Qaoud	gospelrelevance.com
David Simon	davidsimononline.com
James Williams	growingingrace.blog
Jess Bird-Bellis	jessbirdbellis.com
Jessica Head	jessicahead.com
Kris Sinclair	krissinclair.com
Lacey Labs	laceyreapsomephotography.com
Madelyn Canada	thecornershelf.com
Nicholas Lewis	thescribblingscribeblog.com

Nitoy Gonzales	delightinggrace.wordpress.com
Noah Gwinn	instagram.com/ntgwinn
Ruth Baker	whereiam.blog
Stacie Van de Weghe	basicallyamazing.net
Tim Pollock	323academy.com/323-blog
Zach Barnhart	zachbarnhart.com

And to our Heavenly Father who puts his kids' posts on his fridge: thank you. We offer up all of these words for your glory.

Made in the USA
Coppell, TX
12 November 2020

41239559R00111